Rethinking Higher Education

Series Editors

Jeanne Marie Iorio, Melbourne Graduate School of Education, The University of Melbourne, Melbourne, VIC, Australia

Clifton S. Tanabe, The University of Texas at El Paso, El Paso, TX, USA

The current state of higher education perpetuates fatalism, where choice and decision-making towards equity and change has been replaced with bottom-lines and return on investment. This series disrupts this present state of higher education by sharing the stories, actions, and research of students, academics, and administrators in higher education that begin with humanity, equity, and change. It highlights the work of scholars at all stages of career (emerging, mid-career, senior) as well as students beginning their experiences in higher education. Edited, single-authored, and co-authored texts all contribute to new discussions around what is possible in higher education when students, academics, and administrators push their capacity to create possibilities grounded in the ethical and political. This series offers a variety of provocations to rethink teaching, research, policies, and procedures in higher education and working towards local and global change and engagement.

More information about this series at http://www.springer.com/series/16311

Jeanne Marie Iorio · Clifton S. Tanabe

Higher Education and the Practice of Hope

Foreword by William Ayers

 Springer

Jeanne Marie Iorio
Melbourne Graduate School of Education
The University of Melbourne
Melbourne, VIC, Australia

Clifton S. Tanabe
College of Education
The University of Texas at El Paso
El Paso, TX, USA

ISSN 2662-1479 ISSN 2662-1487 (electronic)
Rethinking Higher Education
ISBN 978-981-13-8644-2 ISBN 978-981-13-8645-9 (eBook)
https://doi.org/10.1007/978-981-13-8645-9

© Springer Nature Singapore Pte Ltd. 2019
This work is subject to copyright. All rights are reserved by the Publisher, whether the whole or part of the material is concerned, specifically the rights of translation, reprinting, reuse of illustrations, recitation, broadcasting, reproduction on microfilms or in any other physical way, and transmission or information storage and retrieval, electronic adaptation, computer software, or by similar or dissimilar methodology now known or hereafter developed.
The use of general descriptive names, registered names, trademarks, service marks, etc. in this publication does not imply, even in the absence of a specific statement, that such names are exempt from the relevant protective laws and regulations and therefore free for general use.
The publisher, the authors and the editors are safe to assume that the advice and information in this book are believed to be true and accurate at the date of publication. Neither the publisher nor the authors or the editors give a warranty, expressed or implied, with respect to the material contained herein or for any errors or omissions that may have been made. The publisher remains neutral with regard to jurisdictional claims in published maps and institutional affiliations.

This Springer imprint is published by the registered company Springer Nature Singapore Pte Ltd.
The registered company address is: 152 Beach Road, #21-01/04 Gateway East, Singapore 189721, Singapore

Foreword

The Thing with Feathers
Written by William Ayers

*"Hope" is the thing with feathers—
That perches in the soul—
And sings the tune without the words—
And never stops—at all—*
—Emily Dickinson

This is a book about hope—intrepid, indefatigable, tenacious, constant. It's about that thing with feathers that's permanently perched inside every human soul, ceaselessly singing its songs of freedom and possibility, sometimes muted, other times full-throated. Can you hear it? Can you see it? Picture a sparkling hummingbird, all the colors of the most luminous rainbow, its tiny incandescent wings going 80 beats a second. It's there, vibrating next to your heart, urging you to wake up, eager to inspire your next steps.

This is a book that's not afraid to peer into the abyss, to acknowledge the gathering darkness and the growing intensity of the storms buffeting our shores, to look unstintingly at the world as it is, damaged and dangerous, even as it refuses to be caught in its thrall.

This is a book that proposes courage in the face of fear, hope in opposition to indifference, and action as an antidote to despair.

Audacity, audacity, audacity.

But hope should not be confused with optimism. Optimists think they know what's up ahead—everything will work out for the best, they say, so don't worry, be happy. Like pessimists, their gloomy cousins, optimists embrace determinism, a philosophy that posits a stubborn history leading to an immutable future. The road is already built and laid out before us, the determinists believe, and our journeys are on automatic pilot. Optimists and pessimists share an attitude—a resigned shrug—and a weary phrase: What're you going to do?

Hope exists in an entirely different register. To be hopeful is to recognize that the future is both unknown and unknowable—that I am what I am not yet. It's to remember that the day before every revolution in history, the common opinion was that radical change was impossible, and that the day after, revolution was said to have been inevitable. It's to identify the incompleteness in both oneself, and in the world; it's to name the obstacles to one's (or to our proximate strangers') full humanity; it's to note those things that are out of balance or in need of repair. "Imagination lights the slow fuse of possibility," says Emily Dickinson, and hope is that sizzling fuse. I choose hope precisely because I don't know what's next.

While hope offers no guarantees, it does incite us to action. Because we don't know—and since nothing is inevitable—what we do or what we fail to do matters. And moved to act we begin to look more closely at the world as it is, and then imagine what our shared world should be or could become—utopian visions and freedom dreams begin to appear. Idealism doesn't have to mean innocence or naiveté—we can be experienced and knowledgeable and still insist on nourishing our radical imaginations and elaborating our ideals.

Eduardo Galeano issues a challenge to utopian thinking: *What good is utopia?* he asks. *If I walk two steps toward utopia, it walks two steps away; if I walk ten steps forward, it walks ten steps in the other direction. What good is utopia?* His answer: *It's good for walking.* Yes, a world without manacles appeared in the minds of many long before abolition took hold. And they talked that way, and walked that way.

The rhythm of activism is simple to say, and excruciatingly difficult to enact day-by-day: open your eyes, wake up, and pay attention; be astonished at the beauty in all directions as well as the unnecessary suffering all around; act on whatever the known demands of you; doubt, rethink, and start again.

People resist activism, saying, "I can't do everything." True, no one can. But can you do anything? Anything is where we begin. Or, "I'm only one person, and what can one person do?" The first thing one person can do, of course, is to stop being one person, to reach out and become two, three, many people—a public.

We get involved when we experience the immense latent power of ordinary people rising. There's enormous power in proximity. We link arms and discover the beauty of solidarity—a far cry from "service." We experience the exhilaration of trying *together* to overcome some obstacle to humanity's fullest expression; we grow our souls, suffering setbacks with one another, face-to-face; we act to influence and to learn and to become more complete. We want to win, of course, but the calculus of activism includes the development of our own identity, our deeper humanity. We get involved in activism because there is *no example of justice achieved* without risk, courage, discomfort.

Social justice is a compelling and layered term, not easily or neatly defined, not a destination so much as a journey, a process, a quest. Allowing for fluidity and flexibility, social justice can be thought of as the striving by human beings in different times and places, under vastly different circumstances, typically outside of government and regular politics but necessarily engaging them, and using various tactics and tools and strategies to realize greater fairness, equity, freedom, agency, mobility, participation, and recognition.

Freedom, too, is more complicated and difficult than the easy assumptions that surround it. Isn't freedom a universal aspiration, something that each of us—and everyone we know or have ever heard about—values and desires, a condition that equals happiness and peace-of-mind?

Well, not so fast. Freedom also means risk and responsibility, precariousness and ambiguity. Jean-Paul Sartre tells a story of a graduate student coming to him in occupied France during World War II with a fearsome and formidable dilemma: "My mother is deathly ill," the student explains, "and I'm responsible for her care, but my father is collaborating with the Nazis, and in order to account for that crime I feel I must join the Resistance; what should I do?" After much consideration and discussion of pros and cons, Sartre says, *It seems that you must choose.* The student is unsatisfied: "You're the great philosopher, sir! You should help me choose." *Well,* Sartre continues, *that is precisely the difficulty of every authentic choice, in fact, the problem of freedom—every yes is a no, every no, a yes, and you yourself— no one else—are responsible. You must choose.* "You've been no help to me at all!" says the furious student. "I will go instead to a priest!" Sartre responds, *Very well... which priest will you choose?* We pick our priests, it turns out, to take the terrible gift of freedom off our own heads, to disperse it, or to blame the consequences of our choices on another—but still we choose!

Guarantees of happiness, peace-of-mind, and bread crackle with tension against notions of freedom which, according to Fyodor Dostoevsky's Grand Inquisitor, "men in their simplicity and their natural unruliness cannot even understand, which they fear and dread." This conflict resonates as fundamental—we human beings find ourselves longing for certainty in an uncertain world, something we can hold onto and believe in together, answers to our doubts, perhaps, a single vaccine for the latest virus, the Truth in some final and unquestionable form. We have difficulty tolerating anything as vague and enigmatic as freedom, and this points to the universal allure of dogma and orthodoxy. The insistent message everywhere in society is this: acquiesce, conform, play the game—yes, accede, and perhaps you can call it freedom.

For each of us there is the condition of being, in Hannah Arendt's words, "free and fated, fated and free." We are not entirely determined, but neither do we enjoy absolute liberty and unrestricted choice. No one chooses their parents, to take an obvious example, or their moment in the light; no one chooses a nation or a tribe to be born into. Like everyone else we are situated; and we are free. Thrust into a going world, a world not of our making, we choose (and closing our eyes tight, refusing to see any options whatsoever, is itself a kind of choice) against that hard background of facts.

Today talk of freedom is pervasive in every realm, and everywhere—free trade and the free world, free markets, and free exchange—but it can feel abstract, a given that is both ubiquitous and distant, assumed but not available for active or concrete participation. Personal freedom—our self-proclaimed and celebrated rights and choices, our assumed autonomy and insistent independence—is similarly saturating but strangely off: free to drive anywhere, we find ourselves stuck in traffic; free to speak our minds, we don't have much to say; free to choose, we feel oddly entangled; free to vote for any candidate, we too-often experience a Tweedledum/Tweedledee befuddlement. Most of us, of course, are also entirely dependent on others for a living; we have no voice and no vote in what will be produced, why or how. We experience as well the flattening and pacifying effects of a mass consumer society, the sense of being manipulated, lied to, shaped and used by powerful forces. We hear all around us market fundamentalists defending their "freedom" to extract profits through capitalist markets unfettered by public input or government regulation, all the while promoting the idea that the purest forms of freedom and democratic living can be easily reduced to a question of shopping.

"Freedom Now!" was the call-to-arms of the Black Freedom Movement fifty years ago, and the battle cry of every anti-colonial and anti-imperialist liberation struggle throughout the world in the Twentieth Century. Those movements embraced demands for individual liberties—the right to vote, to access public goods and resources, to live and eat and sit and drink water where one wished—but always within a larger vision of collective freedom, freedom for a community, or for an entire people. Similarly, "women's liberation" and "gay liberation" movements brought a self-identified "public" into being through the process of fighting oppression, discrimination, ill-treatment, or abuse faced by people on the basis of their membership in that particular group or community. Freedom and liberation meant resistance to exploitation and oppression, the possibility of becoming more fully realized human beings with agency and the social power to participate without restriction.

But "freedom" is a wildly contested word, and it is widely and commonly used today to mean personal freedom or the right to do what you want—a far cry from the social meaning of freedom to those various liberation movements. "Freedom" is heralded by leaders of the gig economy and the new libertarian tech culture—Uber is freedom! Facebook is freedom!—as well as members of the ultra-right Freedom Caucus in the US House of Representatives.

In Boots Riley's dazzling film "Sorry to Bother You" a corporation called "Worry Free" promises customers free food and housing, and freedom from the stress of paying bills in return for a lifetime work contract—sound tempting? It's actually modern-day slavery wearing the congenial mask of freedom and cleverly marketed to appeal to folks bathed in the blood of our pervasive consumer culture. "Freedom," remember, was also the motto of the Confederacy—organized traitors willing to burn down the whole house in pursuit of a single "freedom": their presumed right to own other human beings. And "freedom" is the cry of every carbon extractor, invader and occupier, and sweat-shop operator today.

Oh, freedom.

Chicago, Illinois   William Ayers

Preface

This book is not your typical academic text. If you are expecting the usual introduction, methods, results, and discussion, you will not find any of those sections here. Rather, this text is meant as a provocation, a challenge to you as the reader, to engage in what could be and not be stuck in what is. We know higher education is different in our present time. And we have witnessed in our short times as academics, huge structural and policy changes that have impacted the very nature of what higher education is for us and the public. So for us, writing this text was a necessity. A necessity because of the need to disrupt what higher education has become. Underpinning this necessity is hope and this hope has become our "practice of hope." This text is our practice of hope.

We want to empower you as the reader and so in this preface, we share how we have brought together the many parts of our writing. Central to the text is our process of engaging with *A Modest Proposal,* a satirical essay written by Jonathan Swift in 1729 as a means of provoking England and Ireland into taking action to address poverty. We use *A Modest Proposal* and re-write parts of essay in terms of higher education. Each chapter begins by making visible an absurdity within higher education through our re-imagined *A Modest Proposal*. These absurdities function as a way to share the current state of higher education and connect to real-world examples. But is through the practice of hope, we challenge this present construction of higher education and begin to see what could be possible. Our practice of hope is why we share stories and experiences of ourselves and our colleagues around the world that are using the practice of hope. These stories and experiences see higher education as something other than what is too often the norm, a structured business intent on making profit with little regard for the public good. What you will note is that in our writing of the stories, we often use present tense. This is deliberate as we want to bring the readers to these moments of possibility and action. The use of the present tense helps us to do this and we hope helps you to imagine yourself in the stories and seeing that maybe there is space for you to act as well.

Melbourne, Australia Jeanne Marie Iorio
El Paso, USA Clifton S. Tanabe

Contents

1	**A Modest Proposal Re-imagined: How this Work Began**	1
	An Idea	4
	The Structure of this Book	5
	Data Informing the Text	6
	Moving Outside the United States: A Research Project	7
	Stories that Inform and Challenge	8
	An Unexpected Story	8
	References	10
2	**Our Practice of Hope**	13
	Dark Times, Neoliberalism, and Higher Education	14
	Problematizing Neoliberalism in Education Research	14
	Neoliberalism	15
	New Neoliberalism in the Trump Era?	17
	Neoliberalism in Higher Education	18
	A Call to Action	20
	The Practice of Hope	20
	Understanding Hope in the Practice of Hope	21
	Disrupting and Rethinking: Moving Beyond to the Other and Outside	23
	The Practice of Hope in Action: Public Intellectuals in the University	24
	What/Who/Where is the Public in the Public Intellectual?	26
	Technology, Public, and the Anti-public Intellectual	27
	Why the Practice of Hope Now More Than Ever?	28
	References	29
3	**Student as Public Intellectual**	35
	Returning to Story of the Development Course	38
	Disrupting the Absurd: Rethinking the Student as Public Intellectual	39

	Story 1: Early Childhood at University of Hawai'i-West Oahu	41
	Story 2: Early Childhood at Victoria University	44
	Description 3: Activist Educators Engaging Listening, Dialogue, and Action	45
	Disrupting the Absurd: Rethinking Structures and Policies to Support Students as Public Intellectuals	47
	References	53
4	**Academic as Public Intellectual**	**55**
	Back to Being a Waitress	56
	Further Commitments to Neoliberalism	57
	Disrupting the Absurd: The Academic as Public Intellectual	58
	Wide-Awake, Committed, and a Collective	59
	Wide-Awake and Writing	61
	Relevant Issues in the Field Discussed	61
	Commentaries as Provocation	63
	Commentary Writing Building a Collective	63
	Wide-Awake and Researching	64
	Storying: Impact and Engagement with Issues of Social Justice	65
	Out and About: Local and Global Issues of Sustainability	65
	Wide-Awake and Committed to the Public Good	66
	In Australia: The Brisbane Declaration	66
	In the United States: CReATE	68
	In United States: Leaders for the Next Generation	69
	Story 1: A Collective of Public Intellectuals Disrupting and Rethinking Policies and Structure at Victoria University, Australia	70
	Collective Publications	71
	Collective Rethinking Course Outcomes	72
	The Collective Engages with the Conceptual to Disrupt and Rethink	73
	Disrupting the Absurd: Rethinking Structures and Policies to Support Academics as Public Intellectuals	75
	References	80
5	**Administrator as Public Intellectual**	**85**
	Hope and Resistance to Neoliberalism	86
	Another Story	87
	Higher Education Administrator as Manager	88
	Managerialism	89
	Managerialism and Higher Education	89
	Disrupting the Absurd: Rethinking the Administrator as Public Intellectual	91
	Story 1: Young Administrators, Leadership, and the Public Good	92
	Story 2: Administrator Making Spaces for Students and Academics as Public Intellectuals	93

	Story 3: Administrator Making Space to Move Beyond the University	96
	Disrupting the Absurd: Rethinking Structures and Policies to Support Administrators as Public Intellectuals	97
	References	102
6	**The Practice of Hope Across the University**	**103**
	Description 1: School of Social Transformation	104
	School of Social Transformation	104
	A Story: Acting as Public Intellectual Within and Beyond the School of Social Transformation	107
	Local to Global Justice Organization and Annual Gathering	108
	Thinking with Social Justice—Coursework and Action Coming Together	110
	Description 2: Bachelor of Arts	111
	Description 3: A Proposal to Working Across Disciplines	113
	Disrupting the Absurd: Rethinking Structures and Policies to Support Working Across the University	114
	References	118
7	**How to Rethink Your University**	**121**
	Why This Story?	123
	How Might This Look?	124
	Returning Back to Our Modest Proposal	126
	References	127

Chapter 1
A Modest Proposal Re-imagined: How this Work Began

> It is a melancholy object to those who walk through our universities doors and see students developing philosophies on life, critically participating with local and global communities, and graduating citizens willing to question, disrupt, and rethink—these student challenged by academics providing spaces to consider and resist and administrators making and enforcing policies supporting equality and the pursuit of meaning. Instead of perpetuating the status quo, these students, academics, and administrators choose this life in higher education as a site where being aware and attentive to the world is the purpose.
>
> We think it is agreed by all those who are wealthy and in power that the number of thinkers populating universities is in a deplorable state, a very additional grievance. Therefore, whoever could make a method of making these students, academics, and administrators docile members of the university and then society would be recognized as as a hero by those wealth-driven decision-makers.
>
> But our intention is not limited to students, academics, and administrators; it is of a much greater extent, and shall address the very institute of higher education with the faux intention of offering opportunity towards equity. Education at university hath been viewed as the one institution that could disrupt class structures and poverty. We are fully aware of this power within higher education and therefore, making decisions and policies that do not harness this power. Hence harmony in higher education is needed, ensuring representation of perspectives furthering free-market alongside those ever-present radical views. This assures the presence of corporate interest under the guise of a fair and balanced stance across the context of the university.
>
> As privileged decision-makers, many years, writing, misreading data and thus manufacturing crisis and positioning the university as a site of contention. We have thought about ourselves and our success, always finding the work

> *of education scholars within higher education grossly mistaken in their computations. It is true, a student, academic, or administrator, may be a critical contributor to the local and global communities, but for us, the value of these members of higher education is moot. We propose building a system, unaware of what can be possible in the world, measurable through satisfaction, and in terms of the bottom-line. By supporting students, academics, and administrators only as contributors to the market, we as the privileged will continue to thrive.*

We were always an unlikely pair of collaborators. Our partnership first begins as we, two faculty members from separate campuses in different fields, meet over coffee at a local cafe. It is so hot on this day, of course Hawai'i is a warm place, but for some reason, this cafe seems to be the hottest spot on Oahu. Our table presses up against the far wall of the cafe, capturing the heat and radiating it down on our conversation. Beads of sweat on both of our brows, we talk about our work and our writing. Clif, an educational foundations associate professor and lecturer in the law school, is sitting near the kitchen and counter of the cafe. Jeanne Marie, an early childhood associate professor, is sitting with her back towards the open side of the cafe, large, leafy greens behind her in the landscape. Out of this conversation, our first project together emerges and a plan is hatched for our next meeting, definitely in an air-conditioned space.

Clif is central to a grassroots level K-12 teacher listening campaign lead by a local group, hoping to give public school teachers a louder and more authentic voice. His passions towards activism and advocacy evident as he describes the listening and feedback process, inciting ground policy activism through this teacher listening campaign. His desires and intentions to engage with key early childhood policy issues regarding educational equity through this campaign, limited by his knowledge of early childhood expertise. Jeanne Marie's education, experiences, research and writing are the skills needed to fill the gap and offer a way to further the listening campaign.

This moment marks something unique to our work and the connection that traverses our differences—we both recognised our responsibility as members of higher education to engage beyond the doors of our offices and the halls of our departments, to understand the link between policy, practice, and equity, and to respond to the fact that teaching is always political.

This link becomes our reason for gathering. Questions and uncertainty challenge us to consider places and perspectives that are only common to our collaboration. And then an issue is placed on the table for us—the proposed establishment of a state-funded 4-year-old early childhood program in Hawai'i. Not an uncommon proposal for the time, as across the United States this issue is populating many legislative sessions as federal grants and possible funding schemes become available. Economist James Heckman's name and work is dropped all over the place, regardless of context—investing in early childhood is the way to solve all of societal ills. The governor of Hawai'i creates an early childhood office, hires a staff, and funds the writing of a statewide early childhood program. Several bills emerge including a bill to change the constitution in Hawai'i to funnel public funds into private entities. This move essentially supporting the privatization of education. In Hawai'i, there are a handful people with doctorates in early childhood and not one of them is consulted on the proposed early childhood system. Rather, people in the private sector of business and early childhood are leading the charge.

Within all of this flurry, Clif moves his position within the university. After completing a year as the American Council on Education (ACE) fellow during 2013–2014, he is now the Assistant to the Chancellor at University of Hawai'i at Mānoa. Positioning us in different sectors now—a faculty member and an administrator—our unlikely collaboration is now made even more unlikely. The implied separation between administrator and faculty member is the lore of higher education. How can an administrator and a faculty member ever come together? The faculty member is the idealist, the dreamer, the activist. The administrator is the manager, the realist, the budget trimmer. We ignore these assumptions.

Our first act of ignoring is a commentary in *Teachers College Record,* "Fear + Manipulation = Ease of Privatization"—a 1500-word discussion of the public-private solution in order to create the statewide early childhood program to 'ready' children for primary school. We discuss the proposed change to the Hawai'i constitution, how children have been used to advocate for the amendment, and the consequences if the amendment passes. At the same time, we challenge the readers to consider what real work needs to be done in order create an equitable state-funded early childhood program—what happens when you really roll-up your sleeves and do the work rather than create fear and only one solution? The commentary is passed around Hawai'i on emails through colleagues, supporters, and people in disagreement. It is printed on local blogs and in local online news sources. Our opinions are out there, moving through the community. The amendment does not pass.

While we recognise that our influence on the outcome of the amendment may have been minimal, we do note how we can use our position within higher education and as scholars in the field, to bring another perspective to the public. Being public regarding issues like these is powerful because then the ideas, questions, and discomforts all can be discussed. Utilizing the commentary space is different than working within the usual educational research journal genre as the commentary is accessible beyond the higher education community—and it gives a space for our unlikely collaborations.

What we also realise in our process is that underlying our collaborative practices is the ever-present layer of discomfort, anger, and disgust. Put plainly, we are pissed off. We are pissed off at the short-sightedness of policymakers. We are pissed-off by how costs and budgets become the primary criteria for how educational decisions are made. We are pissed-off when universities support and develop programs that only exist to accept federal monies and perpetuate federal dogmas. And then we read the "Tenth Annual *Brown* Lecture in Education Research: A New Civil Rights Agenda for American Education" (Orfield, 2014) in *Educational Researcher*. There in front of us, the list of ridiculous educational decisions is in print. We read and re-read. And we are just pissed-off.

An Idea

Jonathan Swift's *A Modest Proposal* (1729) engages with the mistreatment of Ireland by England through the use of heavy tax burdens on the Irish for use of land owned by England. Famine and the inability to compete with England left the Irish with no opportunities to better their economic situation. This pissed Swift off and so he suggested several reforms which were ignored leading to his original work *A Modest Proposal*. This writing offers the solution to poverty of the Irish by selling their children as food for the wealthy. The absurdity and shock are meant to shame England and Ireland into taking action. What if we re-write Swift to show everyone the absurdity of past educational policies?

Absurdity and shock are needed now. Both of us agree that the current educational policies and practices in the United States are meant to perpetuate the status quo—leaving those with no privilege any choice and continuing that those with privilege have advantage. This indifference and acceptance of our present educational policy practices and the robotic and thoughtless implementation of these policies by public school administrators, teacher educators, and now higher education, enrages us. We have questioned and held discussions with legislators, administrators, and colleagues to build reform that disrupts the status quo and increases privilege beyond the expected. Yet, our proposals fall on deaf ears and the blind servitude to power and profit continues with little or no desire for educational equity. This so evident in our recent involvement in the proposed privatisation of education in Hawai'i. So like Swift, we are pissed-off.

Slowly we begin to re-imagine *A Modest Proposal* considering different educational policies, laws, and actions as absurdity and writing them into our version of A Modest Proposal,

A Modest Proposal Re-Imagined:

For preventing equity within schooling and ensuring the status quo continues (imagined from the perspective of those with power and privilege)

It is a melancholy object to those, who walk through our country's cities, or travel in the rural landscapes, when they see the streets, the sidewalks, the shelters crowded with the poor, families of many races living on the streets in tents, boxes, and carrying their possessions in plastic bags and borrowed grocery carts, importuning those of privilege for money and the government for handout programs. Instead of working, these poor, these others choose this life with little or no desire to move beyond their current situation. And we realize poverty is the source of most of the problems within the education system (Berliner, 2013)—but we ignore this in order to further our own agenda of privilege and power.

…..There is likewise another great advantage to our plan, that it will prevent the development of an education system built on equity, and continue the practice of inequitable schools,

alas! barely meeting the rights of every children (according to the United Nations), honestly more to avoid the expense than the right to an education based on equal opportunity to develop abilities, judgment, and responsibility. To ensure that our plan is not disrupted, we will petition the Court to prevent the extension of affirmative action law and the principles of educational diversity and equal opportunity to K-12 education (Parents Involved in Community Schools v. Seattle School District No. 1, 551 U.S. 701 (2007). Further, we will create a fear campaign focused on the lack of skills of American students, stating these children will never be able to perform in the workplace or the global arena in order to support the market of education through standards, sanctions, school takeovers, prescribed curriculum, and standardized testing. Whereas, many people will gain success from this campaign (at least monetarily) but not those children, the ones outside of advantage, hence they do not contribute to the market and are unimportant to us.

....A very worthy student (by this we mean already privileged and advantaged), a true lover of his country, and whose virtues we highly esteem, will be given multiple opportunities to learn and become leaders upon this scheme. While we know it is illegal to discriminate based on race, we use the ability to discriminate by location to the best of our abilities. And we use this awareness of the lack of resources for parents and families to have access to the neighborhoods and schooling that might further mobility beyond poverty in order to ensure the true goal, we confess, of education that hath always been—perpetuating the status quo. (Iorio & Tanabe, 2015)

This version of our re-imagined *A Modest Proposal* considers schooling across the years in the United States and leads us to believe neoliberalism is the reason for all the absurdity in the education system. It is here where we draw inspiration for this text. Through the act of re-imagining *A Modest Proposal* again, we focus this time only in terms of higher education. Further, this is where our practice of hope (Iorio & Tanabe, 2015) emerges from as neoliberalism has produced a fatalistic context in education, omnipresent in the daily actions in our universities. Hope for us is the way to disrupt and rethink. Practicing hope is how we choose to be in higher education. Hope is our responsibility as educators and how we engage as "provocateurs" taking "a stand while rejecting involvement in either cynical relativism or doctrinaire politics" (Giroux, 2007, p. 38).

The Structure of this Book

As we stated in the Preface, this book is not your typical academic text. Each chapter in this text begins with a section of the re-imagined *A Modest Proposal* discussing neoliberalism in the context of higher education, including specific stakeholders (students, academics, administrators), the system, and rethinking the university. Neoliberalism in general and specifically to higher education is described in Chap. 2. Following this description, we articulate our practice of hope through theories of hope. We then share one possible way to practice hope—rethinking students, academics, and administrators in higher education as public intellectuals. This is inspired by the many scholars framing the public intellectual within education and higher education (Cushman, 1999; Fraser & Taylor, 2016; Giroux, 1988; 2004; 2006; 2010; Goodson, 1999; Greene, 1978, 1995, 2000, 2005; Lynch, 2006).

Specifically, we focus on Said's (1996) description of the public intellectual as the foundation of this practice of hope,

> someone whose place it is to publicly raise embarrassing questions, to confront orthodoxy and dogma (rather than to produce them) to be someone who cannot be easily co-opted by governments or corporations and who raison d'être is to represent all those people and issues that are routinely forgotten or swept under the rug.
>
> (p. 11)

It also sets up the next three chapters in the text as we rethink the student, academic, and administrator as public intellectual.

Each of these chapters focused on the student, academic, and administrator as public intellectual first share literature and current policies and practices that reflect the neoliberal context of the university. Then, examples of programs, research, and stories reflecting the construct of the public intellectual are included as ways to think about how our ideas can be implemented. We end the chapter with specific ways to rethink policy and structures in the university in order to engage beyond neoliberalism.

Through most of the text, we focus on colleges of education in these chapters as this is our expertise. Schools/colleges/departments of education within the university are directly connected to many government policies and mandates as well as accreditation (sometimes multiple accreditations) in order to function. For example, as federal and state standards drive the education in early childhood through secondary schools, teacher education programs and accreditation requirements are revised to reflect these standards. This offers a complexity to our theories and practices that might not always be part of a department or college beyond education. We do believe the ideas and inspirations discussed in this text are possible across the university so in Chap. 6 we share examples beyond schools/colleges/departments of education, aware of how the commitment to students, academics, and administrators as public intellectuals can structure programs and policies across a university.

The final chapter of the text shares the story of an education system built on hope and practicing ethical and political pedagogies. This system is about the connection between school and the local and global community. Through this story, we summarise the text, consider what we have discussed, and challenge readers to implement a practice of hope. Our intention is to inspire and for people to just begin this work. Beginning may be small, but small moves build mass movement towards change.

Data Informing the Text

Beyond inclusion of relevant literature, we have two sources of data constructing the text. The first is a research project *Rethinking Structures and Policies with the VU Early Childhood Course* at Victoria University, Melbourne, Australia and the second, a group of stories informally collected through conversations with colleagues across the field internationally. Both are further articulated below. The literature, research project, and stories are weaved throughout chapters as examples and possibilities.

Through our re-writing, re-telling, re-storying, we seek to challenge the accepted discussions, practices, and conclusions about higher education, interrogating this false sense of "truth" so easily part of the current educational discourse. We are inspired by the words of Pinedo-Burns (2015 in Iorio & Parnell (Eds.), 2015), "The act of writing is a final act of representation; but as important, writing is a process, a way of wondering, reasoning, connecting, questioning, creating, illustrating, and representing" (p. 167). Through writing, we present new possibilities of change in the policies and structures for consideration situated from our positions in higher education, hoping to "interrogate and make productive use of our privileged position as educators and researcher" (Authers, Groenevald, Jackson, Mundal, & Steward, 2007, p. 311). The process of writing of stories gives us a means to wonder and challenge how we are defining and re-defining our practice of hope. We position the student, academic, and administrator as public intellectual as an act of practicing hope. It is through this re-positioning that we thread ideas and elements necessary for practicing hope by rethinking policies and structures in the university context.

Moving Outside the United States: A Research Project

In 2015, Jeanne Marie moved from Hawai'i to Australia for a job. Since this work had been so pivotal to both Clif and Jeanne, when she arrived at her new university, the practice of hope came along with her. Her new group of colleagues in the early childhood program willing took on the practice of hope and developed a research project documenting the practice of hope in rethinking the undergraduate and graduate program in early childhood/primary education. Jeanne and Clif work as co-principal investigators on the project *Rethinking Structures and Policies with the VU Early Childhood Course* seeking to challenge the accepted discussions, practices, and conclusions about early childhood education that are part of the course. This includes interrogating single 'truths' so easily part of the current early childhood discourse (for example, developmental milestones, activity-based teaching) and rethinking the structures and policies governing the course (for example, course outcomes and traditional lecture/tutorial structures). The project uses both writing as a method (Berger, 2013; Chase, 2005; Leavy, 2009; Pinedo-Burns, 2015) for understanding and document review (Hodder, 1994) as the primary sources of data collection.

Data gathered was analyzed using Latour's (2005) notions of tracing, assembling, and paying attention to gatherings of ideas, conversations, contestations, and documents created through the process of rethinking the program by the researchers. These actions are viewed through the frame to disrupt any commitment to a fixed and changeless knowledge of, in this case, the context of higher education. Rather, these actions break the over-reliance on neoliberalism and support a shift towards choices that complexify practice focused on the commitment to the practice of hope and how it links to policy and structures in the context of this program.

Stories that Inform and Challenge

Throughout the text, we share many stories, engaging in Quintero and Rummel's (2015) research practice of storying with bringing together human experience, creativity, and actions within the university. Storying brings together critical theory and narrative inquiry, noting that story is the means by which complexities may be realized, recognised, and become inspirational" (p. 9). Quintero and Rummel note how story "presents situations, new knowledge and information, and challenges potential in complex, interrelated ways" with complexity connecting, "history, the known and unknown, with current times" (p. 5). This process was very relevant as some of the stories relate to our own personal experiences with policy, structures, and leaderships within higher education.

The story at the start of this chapter is a good example of this and influences how we work with other stories that we have collected in regard to our practice of hope. Much of our collaborations happen in casual conversations outside the university—and we use this same frame in our dialogues with colleagues depicted in some of the stories in the text. We have thought about it as a collective. First a small collective between the both of us. And then a larger collective as we sat with our colleagues and discussed the practice of hope, usually over food and drink. The experience of eating and drinking together support the sociality in these dialogues, creating a space of connecting and sameness where emotions, memories, and stories emerge (Pink, 2008; Walmsley, 2005). This process of storying (Quintero & Rummel, 2015) become the foundation for kinship and affinity where knowledge is shared and unity is created. The building of the collective continues.

An Unexpected Story

Writing to understand, writing to rethink, writing to engage—we continue to work on this text through the September, October, November of 2016—thinking we have all the elements to discuss the relevance and need for this work. In the weeks up to the election, we joke about the possibility of electing Donald Trump, the Republican candidate for the office of the President of the United States. One of us—Jeanne Marie—chats with our editor at Springer in October and the possibility of Trump being president is far-fetched, a long shot. It is not even a consideration of how it might impact this book. And then the unexpected happens. On November 8 2016, Donald Trump becomes the President-elect. Stunned. We cannot believe it. President Trump. It is even hard for us to say. We wonder how our fellow citizens could still vote for a man after all of his racist and sexist actions. But we also realise how now more than ever there needs to action, awareness, disruption, and rethinking.

With approximately only 60% of the people in the United States voting during the 2016 election (http://www.pbs.org/newshour/updates/voter-turnout-2016-elections/), we wonder about the 40%. With new election restrictions, limited polling hours, and general apathy, people did and could not vote (Robertson, 2016). Anti-voting campaigns reflect the intensity of distrust in the electorate left people not voting. And those that cannot vote—"over 6 million current or formerly incarcerated persons, over 11 million undocumented workers, over 4 million residents of "unincorporated" United States imperial territories, at least half a million homeless people, and many many more who were disqualified through aggressive voter suppression and the gutting of the Voting Rights Act" (Ayers, 2016b)—sat silently by while their fate is determined by others. At the same time, we wonder about the people that did vote and their intentions and understandings of the issues impacting their local, national, and international communities. And then we wonder how the commitment to neoliberalism, the success of the individual, and the drive for profit has become how voting and democratic choice is defined.

Our wonderings align with Ayers (2016a) question of "what if?"—"What if? That humble question might be the single spark that can ignite a massive prairie fire, provoking us to leap beyond personal speculation and into the vortex of political struggle and social action" (p. 24). For us, "what if?" becomes part of our practice of hope as it challenges the expected and accepted and imagines the possibilities of our wonderings.

> What if we took a radically different angle of regard and questioned the insistent dogma of common sense? What if we unleashed our wildest imaginations? The "what if" question might then blow open the spectrum of acceptable possibilities and take us down a rabbit hole or up into orbit—onto one of life's restless and relentless journeys, exploring and experimenting, orbiting and spinning, inventing and adapting, struggling toward knowledge and enlightenment, freedom and liberation, fighting to know more in order to do more.
> (p. 24)

For us, what if higher education is the "democratic public sphere" (Giroux, 2006, p. 64) working towards the "common good" (Marginson, 2016) where assumptions can be challenged and rethinking local and global policies and practices begin? In our practice of hope we want to use our "wildest imaginations" to see and act beyond neoliberal limitations of the construct of the university, to scaffold and support people in thinking and acting towards equity. This includes "fighting to know more" about how neoliberalism informs the policies and structures in higher education and how this knowledge can empower people to see the neoliberal practices in the daily lives, beyond the university walls. What if awareness, disruption, and rethinking were what was learned and practiced across higher education? How might the choices of the 60% voting in this past election change? How might the choices of the 40% not voting in the past election change? And how might the 100% make choices that represent those that cannot vote?

We return to Ayers (2016a) as a way to end this chapter and to begin your journey through our ideas. Ayers parallels our desire to provoke, to consider the world today, and how our practice of hope starting in higher education could be an impetus for rethinking and action locally, nationally, and globally as he questions, "What kinds of people do we want to become?" (p. 115). He further challenges us to consider:

- What does it mean to be human right now, today?

- How can we act ethically in our hurried, off-balance, and bewildering world?
- How did we get here, and where do we want to go?
- What is our map of the known world, and how might it look if we rethought it from top to bottom and redrew all the lines?
- What is our responsibility as world citizens to one another and to future generations?
- What kind of society do we want to inhabit?
- What is the relationship of democracy to economics?
- Who do we want to be as people? What can we become?
- What gives meaning to our lives?

Our practice of hope is how we begin to imagine how policies and structures in higher education—a space where students, academics, and administrators explore and understand what it means to be human, how to resist and rethink the known world, articulate our responsibilities to society and a democracy, and to make meaning in relationships that generate ethical practices. Engaging with the practice of hope in higher education empowers people to recognise the power of a humanity that acts toward equity, a humanity that we hope for each day.

References

Authers, B., Groenevald, E., Jackson, E., Mundal, I., & Steward, J. (2007). Engaging academic activism, a preface. *Review of Education, Pedagogy, and Cultural Studies, 29*(4), 311–316.

Ayers, W. (2016a). *Demand the impossible*. Chicago: Haymarket Books.

Ayers, W. (2016b). Posting, December 16. Retrieved from www.billayers.org.

Berger, I. (2013). *Narration-as-action: The potential of pedagogical narration for leadership enactment in early childhood education contexts*. Vancouver: University of British Columbia Library. https://doi.org/10.14288/1.0103380.

Berliner, D. (2013). Effects of inequality and poverty vs. teachers and schooling on America's youth. *Teachers College Record, 115*(12), 1–26

Chase, S. E. (2005). Narrative inquiry: Multiple lenses, approaches, voices. In N. K. Denzin & Y. S. Lincoln (Eds.), *Handbook of qualitative research* (3rd ed., pp. 651–679). Thousand Oaks, CA: Sage.

Cushman, E. (1999). Opinion: The public intellectual, service learning, and activist research. *Service Learning, General*, 84.

Fraser, H., & Taylor, N. (2016). *Neoliberalization, universities and the public intellectual*. New York: Palgrave.

Giroux, H. (1988). *Teachers as intellectuals*. New York: Praeger.

Giroux, H. (2004). Cultural studies, public pedagogy, and the responsibility of intellectuals. *Communication and Critical/Cultural Studies, 1*(1), 59–79.

Giroux, H. (2006). Higher education under Siege: Implications for public intellectuals. *Thought & Action*, 63–78.

Giroux, H. (2007). Utopian thinking in dangerous times: Critical pedagogy and the project of educated hope. In M. Cote, G. de Peuter, & R. Day (Eds.), *Utopian pedagogy: Radical experiments against neoliberal globalization* (pp. 25–42). Toronto: University of Toronto Press.

Giroux, H. (2010). Bare pedagogy and the scourge of neoliberalism: Rethinking higher education as a democratic public sphere. *The Educational Forum, 74*, 184–96.

References

Goodson, I. (1999). The educational researcher as a public intellectual. *British Educational Research Journal, 25,* 277–297.

Greene, M. (1978). *Landscapes on learning.* New York: Teachers College Press.

Greene, M. (1995). *Releasing the imagination: Essays on education, the arts, and social change.* San Francisco: Jossey-Bass.

Greene, M. (2000). The ambiguities of freedom. *English Education, 33,* 8–14.

Greene, M. (2005). Teaching in a moment of crisis: The spaces of imagination. *The New Educator, 1,* 77–80.

Hodder, I. (1994). The interpretation of documents and material culture. In N.K. Denzin & Y.S. Lincoln (Eds.), *Handbook of qualitative research* (pp. 393–402). Thousand Oaks: Sage Publications.

Iorio, J.M., & Tanabe, C.S. (2015). A modest proposal re-imagined: Disrupting and rethinking educational decision-making. *Teachers College Record.* Date Published: December 10, 2015. http://www.tcrecord.org, ID Number: 18828.

Latour, B. (2005). *Reassembling the social: An introduction to actor-network-theory.* New York, NY: Oxford University Press.

Leavy, P. (2009). *Method meets art.* New York, NY: Guilford Press.

Lynch, K. (2006). Neo-liberalism and marketisation: the implications for higher Education. *European Educational Research Journal, 5* (1), 1–17.

Marginson, S. (2016). *Higher education and the common good.* Melbourne, AU: MUP Academic.

Orfield, G. (2014). Tenth annual Brown lecture in education research: A new civil rights agenda for American education. *Educational Researcher, 43*(6), 273–292.

Parents Involved in Community Schools v. Seattle School District No. 1, 551 US 701 (2007).

Pinedo-Burns, H. (2015). Puffins, butterflies, and clouds in the preschool: The importance of wonder. In J. Iorio & W. Parnell (Eds.), *Rethinking readiness in early childhood education: Implications for policy and practice* (pp. 165–178). New York: Palgrave Macmillan.

Pink, S. (2008, June). An urban tour: The sensory sociality of ethnographic place-making. *Ethnography, 9,* 175–196. https://doi.org/10.1177/1466138108089467.

Quintero, E.P., & Rummel, M.K. (2015). *Storying: A path to our future: Artful thinking, learning, teaching, and research.* New York: Peter Lang, Series on Critical Perspectives in Qualitative Research.

Robertson, C. (2016). Millions on election day make a different decision: Not voting. *The New York Times*, November 16. Retrieved from https://www.nytimes.com/.

Said, E. (1996). *Representations of the intellectual: The 1993 Reith lectures.* London, UK: Vintage Books.

Swift, J. (1729). *A modest proposal.* Retrieved from http://www.gutenberg.org/files/1080/1080-h/1080-h.htm.

Walmsley, E. (2005). Race, place and taste: Making identities through sensory experience. *Etnofoor, 18*(1), 43–60.

Chapter 2
Our Practice of Hope

> *We shall now therefore humbly propose our own thoughts, which we hope will not be liable to the least objection. We have been assured by a very knowing privileged male of our acquaintance, that an ideology free of regulation and rules could nourish those with a money-making agenda.*
>
> *We do therefore humbly offer the ideology of neoliberalism to public consideration that deregulation, privatization, removal of government control as sufficient tools to further corporate governance of social programs and assets. Neoliberalism will make it possible for profit to be the purpose of democracy, slowly neoliberalism will move across the public through institutions and settling in higher education.*
>
> *We have reckoned the force of neoliberalism on the context of the university will stop the production of thinking, active citizens and remove this danger to the well-established ruling class of society.*

Writing in response to Hannah Arendt's *Men in Dark Times* (1968), Philosopher Maxine Greene notes Arendt's understanding of the need for light—"a space where in which light can be shed on what is happening and what is being said" (Greene, 1997, p. 1). Arendt's writing refers to the era of Nazi rule in Germany and Greene does not draw comparison with American history but rather sees how "dark times are no rarity" sharing the circumstances of the current time (in this case, 1997), in particular in schools and society, are "shadowed",

> I view our times as shadowed by violations and erosions taking place around us: the harm being done to children; the eating away of social support systems; the "savage inequalities" in our schools; the spread of violence; the intergroup hatreds; the power of media; the undermining of arts in the lives of the young.
>
> (p. 1)

It is interesting how Greene's (1997) descriptions of "shadowed" run parallel to the very state of higher education and the our current state of the world as violence and inequity continue throughout our daily lives. She sees the connection between education and how the world functions; then wonders how this state of affairs might be disrupted. For Greene, this is through the power of imagination, "Imagination, after all, allows people to think of things as if they could be otherwise; it is the capacity that allows a looking through windows of the actual towards alternative realities" (p. 1–2). Greene suggests the actions of teachers as a way to see the light in "dark times" as they engage in the capacity to see what is possible.

We take inspiration from Greene's proposal for teachers, kindling the light of what is possible in higher education during these dark times. Greene's (1997) work is a call to us to consider how imagination might offer a way to see alternative realities— "to think of things as if they could be otherwise" (p. 1). Our re-imagined *A Modest Proposal* engages our imaginations, pushes our capacity to look through a window to an alternate reality of higher education. Through this chapter, we articulate what we see as the "dark times" of higher education influenced by neoliberalism and suggest the practice of hope to "kindle" the light. We further share an example of one way to practice hope by repositioning students, academics, and administrators as public intellectuals.

Dark Times, Neoliberalism, and Higher Education

Neoliberalism runs rampant in higher education (Apple, 2001; Giroux, 2005; 2014; 2016; Marginson, 2016; Saunders, 2011a) creating an environment that perpetuates fatalism. For us, these are "dark times" for higher education. Yet, what is neoliberalism? Understanding the overall neoliberal context—socially, politically, culturally, economically—is essential to understanding the context in higher education.

Problematizing Neoliberalism in Education Research

We begin this section by problematizing neoliberalism as the extensive and vague use of the concept across education leaves it vulnerable to criticism. In educational research, Rowlands and Rowalle (2013) assert that "neoliberalism has come to be used and understood within some parts of academia and in the media as a catch-all explanation for anything negative" (p. 261). They go on to argue,

> The point here is that although neoliberalism is often used as a generic descriptor for right-leaning, negative phenomena, this is not particularly helpful because such usage implies that neoliberalism is a unitary concept which belies the complex and contested nature of the phenomenon. It also does not acknowledge that neoliberalism is only one of the many things influencing contemporary public policy and private practice.

> (Rowlands & Rawolle, 2013, p. 261)

Using the Bourdieuian concept of *illusio* and *doxa*, Rowlands and Rawolle (2013) note that when neoliberalism is always pinned as the usual reason for any negative policy, practice, or situation within educational research, there is further reinforcement of neoliberalism. In other words, we are "playing the neoliberal game and inadvertently demonstrating our belief that it is a game that is worth being played" (p. 270). Through the review of 110 educational research articles utilising the words neoliberal or neoliberalism or neo-liberal or neo-liberalism, Rowlands and Rawolle note when no, brief, and extensive definitions of the concept were offered. The authors respond to the data by sharing how the lack of the complexity in the defining of neoliberalism creates the possibility of being misunderstood. Disruption of "the neoliberal doxa by using the word 'neoliberal' and its variants consciously (indeed, reflexively) and critically in our research" is a means of actively revolting against neoliberalism. This is about making visible "what we mean and for what purpose so that our work has maximum use-value in the ways we might have intended" (p. 270).

We pay attention to this critique of neoliberalism in academe and build our practice of hope in response to first articulating how we understand neoliberalism in general times. Then we detail how we understand neoliberalism within the context of higher education. This explicitly presents what we mean by neoliberalism in higher education and how this contributes to our response and action through the practice of hope. For us, hope is our response to an understanding of neoliberalism and its implications in the university.

Neoliberalism

The term neoliberalism, also known as free market, free trade, or globalization, emerged in 1938 during a meeting in Paris by Ludwig von Mises and Friedrich Hayek. Both took on the perspective that Franklin Roosevelt's New Deal and Britain's welfare state operated "as manifestations of a collectivism that occupied the same spectrum as nazism and communism" (Monbiot, 2016a). Neoliberalism became the way to disrupt these policies reeking of socialism and appealed to the wealthy yearning to break free of regulations and rules limiting their money-making agendas.

In the 1970s, neoliberalism in the United States revitalized laissez faire policies (non-interference by government in free-market capitalism) from the 1930s, but re-imagined in the current economic and social context (Harman, 2008). Embracing American economist Friedman's (1962) understanding of the free market as deregulation, privatization, and cutback, neoliberalism provided a framework for the removal of government regulation in order to make money and usher in an era of corporate control of government assets and social programs, again with the intent of profit.

Essentially, neoliberalism works to situate profit as the purpose of democracy, constructing market as the only way to solve all of the woes of society, without recognition of context and inequity (Giroux, 2014). It "transmogrifies every human domain and endeavour, along with humans themselves, according to a specific image of the economic" (Brown, 2015, p. 9), wearing away the principles, practices, and heart of democracy. Further, neoliberalism expands the idea of the market beyond the economic sphere, and into the social, cultural, and political (Lemke, 2001). Places like schools are now subject to "objective" economic analysis, with little to no recognition of the social importance of these places or the culture constructed through them. Relationships are defined by competition with people as consumers, and democratic choice is maintained through consumption.

Relationships are key to understanding that neoliberalism is everywhere. We are never outside of power. Foucault (1987) reminds us that everyone participates in power relations, "whatever they are—whether it be a question of commnicating verbally...or a question of a love relationship, an institutional or economic relationship—power is always present: I mean the relationship one wishes to direct the behaviour of other" (p. 11). So whether we are speaking about a marriage, government, higher education, or a classroom, power is present and power contributes to how we act and think. This also is how we are shaped to self-govern by what power institutes as the dominant discourse. "Dominate discourses organise our everyday experience of the world, influencing our ideas, thoughts, and actions. They exercise power over our thought by governing what we see as the 'truth', what we accept as rational and how we construct the world—and hence our acting and doing" (Dahlberg & Moss, 2005, p. 18). So when neoliberalism is the dominant discourse driving how we think and act, this becomes how we govern ourselves, termed as "governmentality" (Foucault, Burchell, Gordon, & Miller, 1991).

> These practices work directly on us, steering us towards desired behaviour. But they also work through us, acting on our intermost selves, reaching to the innermost qualities of being human: our spirit, motivations, wishes, desires, beliefs, dispositions, aspirations, and attitudes. So though we are directly governed, the most important effect is that we govern ourselves—conduct of our own conduct—in ways that conform to the dominant regime.
> (Dahlberg & Moss, 2005, p. 19)

In other words, governmentality situates us to take on neobliberalism as our tale of how we live, act, work, and think. This is problematic if we consider what neoliberalims propagates.

Neoliberalism perpetuates fear, manipulates the public, and supports privatisation (Iorio & Tanabe, 2015a), commodification, and deregulation (Giroux, 2014). Journalist Klein (2007) describes the use of shock and coercion as a way to give rise to free market noting how "moments of collective trauma" become the means "to engage in radical social and economic engineering" (Klein, 2007, p. 9). A strong example Klein shares is the rise of the privatization of public schools in New Orleans, Louisiana following the devastation of Hurricane Katrina. With children displaced and schools in ruin, American economist (and staunch supporter of the free market) Friedman (2005) saw this excuse to entirely remake the system of education. This included the privatization of public schools through a voucher system and the establishment of charter schools (Klein, 2007). Further, in the neoliberal context, this solution to the devastation of Hurricane Katrina is positioned as the only way to solve the problem—no alternative can exist.

More recently, we witnessed this in the presidential campaign of Donald Trump as his "doomsaying" became the shock necessary to promote the rise of the free market in his term as president. "Mr. Trump, for his part, spoke of apocalypse now, painting contemporary America as crime-plagued (a claim not especially true) and economically stagnant (a better grounded one), and at the edge of an irreversible decline" (Robertson, 2016). Fear, shock, manipulation, coercion, all part of how Trump was elected. But this "shock doctrine" contributes to the ever-present reality of the world—a "dystopian neoliberal world in which crises are created and manipulated to maintain cynicism and cultivate fear, where violence and dysfunction are commodified and marketed as entertainment, or worse as legitimate political discourse" (Burns, 2016).

Klein (2017) writes, "the incarnation of a still-powerful free-market ideological project" (p. 37), Trump is a "one-man megabrand" with the "embodiment of the belief that money and power provide license to impose one's will on others" (p. 36). This is particularly evident as the privatization of the state and the neoliberal policies of previous political administrations impact the ability to vote in order to change people's circumstances and privilege becomes smaller. With neoliberalism, choice is through consumption and spending—so those with more money have more choice, while those with less money, less choice. Votes are not fairly rationed and politics become irrelevant. This leaves those with less privilege, usually the lower- and middle-class without power and voice, open to anti-politics. It is these people who found a place with Trump and the hope to "make America great again"—a slogan appealing to those disempowered and silenced. "The monumental election of Trump was a desperate and xenophobic cry of human hearts for a way out from under the devastation of a disintegrating neoliberal order—a nostalgic return to an imaginary past of greatness" (West, 2016).

Trump believes that government should both further business and be managed as a business as he "wants the country to be run like his own private country club, is surrounded by hacks and quislings as eager to carry his gilded jock strap as his golf bags" (McLaren, 2016). This is reflected in his choice of filling his cabinet with a group of wealthy elites with a net worth of over $14.5 billion, money often made "by knowingly causing harm to some of the most vulnerable people on the planet, and to the planet itself, often in the midst of crisis" (Klein, 2017, p. 52). So while Trump may have been elected based on how he would work for the disempowered and silenced, his cabinet is not reflective of these people. Rather, his choices imply the possibility of an even more intense form of neoliberalism (Tarnoff, 2016), one that moves beyond humanity and supports the pursuit of profit even if it perpetuates racism, sexism, and oppression.

New Neoliberalism in the Trump Era?

We recognise that the neoliberal economy has benefitted some, but not all. As the middle class continues to get smaller and poorer, and "the all-out war on the public sphere and public interest" (Klein, 2017, p. 22) begins to reveal itself, neoliberalism has begun to lose traction as a persuasive conceptual framework for effective policy. This is evident in the failures of the policies reaching the middle class, multiple economic crisis, elevated costs in education and healthcare, and increased poverty and homelessness. It is not surprising that in the aftermath of the economic meltdown of 2008, Comaroff (2011) asked whether neoliberalism had reached its "natural" end.

With populist backlash in the United States and in other countries (https://www.hrw.org/sites/default/files/world_report_download/wr2017-web.pdf), against international integration, open trade, and globalization, the basic neoliberal tenets no longer seem inevitable (Davies, 2016). And, while Trump seems to operate from a traditional neoliberal position, the populist movement that swept him into office does not. In fundamental ways, populist movements on both the left and right are predicated on the perception that neoliberal ideas and policies have failed. West (2016) captures this sentiment in unvarnished language when he writes, "[t]he neoliberal era in the United States ended with a neofascist bang," and that "the age of Obama was the last gasp of neoliberalism". The "neofacist bang" as West refers to is, of course, the election of Donald Trump, and the triumph of anti-establishment mores.

Neoliberalism in Higher Education

The institution of higher education has alway been conscious of its power to address social inequities and lead the evolution of democracy relevant to the current times—socially, politically, and economically (Giroux, 2016). In the 1960s, universities became a place where students defined their philosophies on life (Astin, 1998), engaged critically with local and global communities, and graduated people as thinkers willing to question (Giroux, 2016). Higher education merged "politics, justice, civil rights, and the search for truth" creating

> a crucial public sphere that held power accountable, produced a vast array of critical intellectuals, joined hands with the anti-war and civil rights movements, and robustly challenged what Mario Savio once called "the machine"—an operating structure infused by the rising strength of the financial elite that posed a threat to the principles of critique, dissent, critical exchange, and a never-ending struggle for inclusivity.
>
> (Giroux, 2016, p. 147)

These actions within higher education at this time threatened the "machine"—in particular, the possible commodification, privatization, and marketization of the university and those in power supportive of neoliberalism. The Powell Memo (23 August 1971) written for the Chamber of Commerce by Lewis F. Powell, Jr., lawyer, corporation board member, and later member of the US Supreme Court, cites colleges campuses as sites of an "assault" on the American economic system (p. 1). He notes how universities are funded and supported by American businesses through taxes, controlled and generated capital gains, and as trustee members on university boards (p. 1). According to Powell, actions demonstrating the assault include faculty on campuses not believing in the enterprise system, often representative of left-wing, Marxist, and socialist perspectives, inclusion of radical speakers to students further offering disbelief in the current American economic system, and graduating students representative of these ideals who move to work in media, government, and business—bringing their disruptive convictions into the workplace. Powell calls for a "balance" in the college of faculty and visiting scholars believing in the American economic system, essentially neoliberalism. Powell's memo illustrates his deep understanding of the power of education to change society, and in his eyes, changing society to further the corporation of America, should be part of the university system. "The Powell Memo was the most influential of a number of ideological interventions in the 1970s that developed political road maps to crush dissent, eliminate tenure, and transform the university into an adjunct of free-market fundamentalism" (Giroux, 2016, p. 168).

Presently in the United States, the reduction of government funding coupled with the deregulation of fees has contributed directly to the context of higher education, commodifying and privatising universities. These same factors are seen beyond the United States; in Australia, neoliberalism has contributed structures within the universities resembling corporations focussing on competition (Marginson 2004, 2016; Marginson & Considine, 2000). Private funding, reliances on part-time faculty, and faculty forced to generate monies through research focused on practical and profit-driven purposes (Mirowski, 2011) are all commonplace to how universities function (Saunders, 2011b). Higher education is now a business, with fees and profit critical to survival. This positions administrators as CEOs, students as consumers, and academics as service providers—all roles contributing to the "edu-factory" (Haiven, 2014) where degrees are purchased and research is for sale (this will be discussed in detail in later chapters). Ranking of universities, performance evaluations, impact and citation counts of publications are the ways in which success is determined—quantitative and narrow in the defining of the academic and the institution. Retention and first-year-experience (Baik, Naylor, & Arkoudis, 2015; Hope, 2017; James, Krause, & Jennings, 2010; Nelson, Kift, & Clarke, 2012; Thomas, 2002; Zepke, 2014) are paramount to teaching and research and the emergence of teaching-only appointments dominate hiring practices (Bexley & Arkoudis, 2013; Billot, 2010; Else, 2015; Larkin, 2011; Probert, 2013, 2014).

The purpose of higher education is repositioned as workforce development (Giroux, 2016) and reeks of consumerism and the intent to train students to become competent consumers furthering a new generation supportive of neoliberalism. "The atomisation and self-interested behaviour neoliberalism promotes run counter to much of what comprises human nature" (Monbiot, 2016b). As universities rethink strategic plans from commitments to equity to increases in student retention and viewing students as customers, human nature is secondary and self-interest is primary. "Education under neoliberalism is a form of radical depoliticization, one that kills the radical imagination and the hope for a world that is more just, equal and democratic" (Giroux in Harper, 2014, p. 1079). Neoliberalism has become the normality of higher education in

> requests for information for various external systems of measurement, in concerns about and celebrations of students numbers, in warnings about any dissatisfactions in our customers, in talk of journal outputs as a proxy of research, and in increasing requests made in the name of the student experience (which range from answering their emails the same day to facilitating frequent satisfaction surveys).
>
> (Molesworth, Scullion, & Nixon, 2010, p. 129)

Students are positioned as commodities making universities sites for "consuming" content, and less about engaging with ideas and working towards social justice, change and humanity. Essentially, a Marcusean one-dimensionality acculturates the university as a "product of an intricate amalgam of capitalism, technology, and instrumental rationality, which penetrate the thought, language, and action of society" (Cunningham, 2016, p. 542). This accepted state of neoliberalism with the university drips of fatalism. This is worrisome and heeds a call to action.

A Call to Action

Our action begins with the practice of hope because "without hope, there is no way we can start thinking about education" (Freire, 2007, p. 87). We recognize that we live in "dark times" as Greene (1997) suggests but at the same time, "we are never freer as teachers and students, citizens, residents, activists and organizers, and artists and thinkers than when we shake ourselves free and refuse to see the situation or the world before us as the absolute end of the matter" (Ayers, 2016, p. 241). We also realise that the "undoing" of neoliberalism is quite complex and entangled as with the presence of neoliberalism, the roots of democracy are remade by economicization (Brown, 2015). Our view is not naïve and we do not think hope is the ultimate solution of "undoing". Rather, we see hope as our way of shaking ourselves free and seeing the university beyond neoliberalism—hope is how we "kindle" the light.

The Practice of Hope

For us, the practice of hope is our way of not giving into the dull and insidious belief that all has been done and our hands are tied in the neoliberal context of higher education. It helps us to imagine what is possible and engage with the impossible. Hope supports us in situating policies and decisions in new experiences, resources, and opportunities rather than bottom-lines, more rules, and narrow views of what should be in higher education. Hope, from a new perspective is not a passive concept. It is not reactive. It is not meditative. Rather, it is defined proactively. Hope as action. Hope as engagement. Hope as responsibility. Hope as a conceptual tool that is capable of replacing accountability as a policy directive. "Hope is a choice, after all, and confidence a politics—our collective antidote to cynicism and despair. It's the capacity to notice or invent alternatives, and then to do something about it, to get busy in projects of repair" (Ayers, 2016, p. 239).

Understanding Hope in the Practice of Hope

In our practice of hope, we see hope as a theoretical tool necessary to rethink higher education, "to reimagine new worlds and create ethical possibilities in practice" (Pacini-Ketchabaw, Nxumalo, Kocher, Elliot, & Sanchez, 2015), to begin with humanity. Hope for our practice is not simply hope as "false hope of one who hopes for the sake of hoping' (Freire, 1978, p. 60). Rather, the practice of hope utilizes "complex hope" (Grace, 1994; Webb, 2010) aware and realistic about the histories, structures, policies, and practices within higher education. We recognise how neoliberalism has supported decontextualized policies and structures, leaving the ethical and political perspectives outside of any related decision-making. Through the use of hope, we want to bring together the technical, conceptual, and the pedagogical into the university, connecting to the communities and population the university serves, while ensuring the inclusion of the ethical and political. This reflects Greene's (1997) perspective on the social and the ethical imagination "concerned for the using ideas and aspirations to reorganise the environment or the lived situation" (pp. 5–6). Teaching is always political and without this recognition, teaching is deskilled and the university is constructed as a place void of thought and engagement. Freire (1992) names "one of the tasks of the progressive education, through a serious, correct political analysis, is to unveil opportunities for hope, no matter what the obstacles may be" (p. 3). Engagement with the ethical and political exposes hope, sees beyond the interference of neoliberalism, and supports the rethinking of higher education through the practice of hope.

Hope is part of who we are as people and it is a logical place where students, academics, and administrators can come together to disrupt and rethink what is accepted in the neoliberal university. Freire (1992, 1998) recognizes hope as a fundamental part of being human while Andrews (2010) notes that "Hope is clearly something humans recognise in themselves and others. It shapes how we view and understand our world and is manifested at many levels" (Andrews, 2010, p. 323). For example, Blas Pedreal (2015) names her work with student affairs in higher education as the practice of hope as a way to counteract the challenges within student affairs. Hope is part of how student affairs personnel and staff support students as well as how hope is encouraged within the students. Blas positions hope as a transformative process and a "catalyst" to her work with students and colleagues—enacting how hope is recognised in her students and colleagues as well as how it shapes her own work within her practice of hope.

We take inspiration on how Freire builds his educational theory on the ontology of hope in our own practice of hope. Freire (1972) notes how "Hope is rooted in men's incompleteness, from which they move out in constant search" (p. 64) and furthers the connection between hope and education as "It is in our incompleteness, of which we are aware, that education as a permanent process is grounded" (Freire, 1998, p. 58). Education for Freire is founded on the search for hope and how humans engage in this search in the awareness of their own incompleteness. In this sense, education becomes the paradigm for hope. Freire's choice to position hope as integral to his educational philosophy eloquently illustrates his understanding of hope that can provide a counter narrative to the fatalism generated by neoliberalism (Freire, 1998). For our practice of hope, higher education can be the guide for hope and the site for humans to engage in the search of hope, recognizing the fundamental connection between hope and education in the university context. This dynamic connection is the means to resist neoliberalism in higher education.

For example, the shift in how students view and engage in higher education demonstrates how neoliberalism has created a context where something is missing. Astin's (1998) study discussing the thirty-year trends (1966–1996) of students in higher education shared how in the 1960s, approximately 75% of the students indicated the reason for attending university was to develop a meaningful philosophy on life while less than a third of the students surveyed noted being financially well-off was an essential purpose of higher education. Thirty years later, developing a meaningful philosophy on life became essential to less than half the students surveyed while over 70% cite a college education as a means to make money. The student shifting from the intrinsic (developing a meaningful philosophy on life) to the extrinsic (making money) constructs a sense of something missing in the current university context. It also may hark to Brown's (2015) notion of how democracy is being remade by neoliberalism as "the commitment to individual and collective self-rule and the institutions supporting it are overwhelmed and then displaced by the encomium to enhance capital value, competitive positioning, and credit ratings" (p. 10).

Hope is addressing the something that is missing, a way to imagine a better world, a future that calls to the present (Bloch, 1995). Hope must be part of the present, in order to imagine the future (Benjamin, 1997; Bloch, 1995; Giroux, 2004; Halpin, 2001; Macquarrie, 1966; Moltmann, 1967). In this sense, hope underpins the practice that moves towards the future with concrete actions within the context of the present—where people act with purpose of creating an improved future. Bloch (1995) offers us the question to consider "What must we dream of?" and it is in this question, we use hope as how we can rethink the university away from its current neoliberal order—a description of the future university.

Bloch (1995) in *The Principle of Hope,* presents a description of the future from a Marxist perspective, positioning utopia as an achievable objective—possible through political decision-making and implementation of socialism. The nature of hope sustains the feasibility of utopia as it makes possible, "something perfect which the world has not yet seen" (p. 14). An utopian perspective offers us two characteristics to consider as it "forces us to consider the idea that, despite present difficulties and past disappointments, an improved way of life can be realised" and epitomizes a "radical, frequently progressive political outlook that undermines old certainties in favour of new, sometimes even unsettling portrayals of a better future" (Halpin, 2001, p. 116). Hope positions people to imagine utopian possibilities, "to look at things as if they could be otherwise" (Greene, 1995, p. 16). Havel (1989) sees hope in the small movements of people gathering together, building relationships as inspiration to new projects, projects working towards change, imagining what could be otherwise. Imagining utopia in higher education offers the opportunity to consider how the university can be constructed outside the neoliberal order. The purpose of addressing social inequities and building (or re-making) democracy becomes primary to how the university functions.

> Hope, in this instance, is one of the preconditions for individual and social struggle, for ongoing practice of critical education at a wide variety of sites; it is also the mark of courage on the part of intellectuals inside and outside of the academy who are using resources of theory to address social problems.
>
> (Giroux in Cote, de Peuter, and Day, 2007, p. 31)

Giroux's understanding of hope is active, rooted in courage—courage to "contest the workings of oppressive power, and undermine various forms of domination" (p. 31). It is action of choosing hope that furthers this courage as Ayers (2016) reminds us,

> Choosing hopefulness is holding out the *possibility* of change. It's living with one foot in the mud and muck of the world as it is, while another foot strides forward toward a world that could be. Hope is never a matter of sitting down and waiting patiently; hope is nourished in action, and it assumes that we are—each and all of us—incomplete as human beings. We have things to do, mountains to climb, problems to solve, injuries to heal. We can *choose* to see life as infused with the capacity to cherish happiness, to respect evidence and argument and reason, to uphold integrity, and to imagine a world more loving, more peaceful, more joyous and more just than the one we were given—and we should.
>
> (p. 240)

Hope is tool for disrupting neoliberalism and through the practice of hope, we can imagine the utopian possibility of what the university can be beyond neoliberalism. Hope responds to what Greene (1997) refers to as the "light in dark times" as hope can be a means to confront the darkness and rethink what could be in higher education.

Disrupting and Rethinking: Moving Beyond to the Other and Outside

The intent to disrupt and think beyond neoliberalism in higher education is not new. For example, Cote et al. (2007) offer utopian pedagogy as a framework to imagine what the university can be through the resistance and rethinking of the limiting structures and policies defined by neoliberalism in higher education. Rooted in anarchism, autonomism, cultural studies, and liberation pedagogy, utopian pedagogy is a radical pedagogical alternative disrupting neoliberalism, striving "to draw out and examine connection between the practices of everyday life and wider structures of domination" (p. 326). Utopian as referred to in this sense is not the fantastical, dream-like, perfect future; rather utopia is viewed as "not as a place we might reach but an ongoing process of becoming" (Cote et al., 2007, p. 13). Utopia is immanent and involves hope as a "temporal vector that points from the present into the future from a specific location, with a determinate direction and force" (Hardt & Negri, 2002, p. 201). Utopian pedagogy is "something *other* than and *outside* of the hyper-inclusive logic of neoliberalism" (Cote et al., 2007, p. 317).

Community-based, self-governed, and free to the public, Critical U. (located in Vancouver, British Columbia) is an example of utopian pedagogy in action. Critical U. offers short classes including social and political theory, globalization, community gardening, and media literacy—topics most pertinent to local community members (Cote et al., 2007, p. 331)—as an alternative to the university context. This community education project offers education *other* than the university (participants do not need to have previous post-secondary experience) and *outside* of the usual structures of a class as grades and rubrics, the conventional written assignments, and expected pedagogies are not present at Critical U. Rather, classes are an active space where pedagogy shifts and morphs depending on the participants choosing to be engaged in this place and topic. Utopian pedagogy and and the example of Critical U. challenge us to think about what could be *other* and *outside* neoliberalism in higher education.

The actions of *other* and *outside* as suggested by Cote et al. (2007) are another means to engage in imagination as Greene (1997) ascribes. The *other* and *outside* are the alternative realities of what the university is and how it functions. The capacity of what can be when we "foster experiments in thinking and acting that lead us away" from neoliberalism in the context of higher education (Cote et al., 2007, p. 332) engages hope to imagine what is *other* and *outside*.

The Practice of Hope in Action: Public Intellectuals in the University

In this text, we offer one example of how to engage the practice of hope by using Cote et al.'s (2007) concept of "thinking and acting" as we want students, academics, and administrators within the university context who can think and act. For us, this calls for students, academics, and administrators to be "wide-awake" in the university. Being "wide-awake" is rooted in Greene's (1995) concept of "wide-awakeness"—an "awareness of what it is to be in the world" (p. 35). "Wide-awakeness" situates "thinking and acting" (Cote et al., 2007) in the reality of the structures, policies, practices, and histories of higher education. Greene's (1977) "wide-awakeness" is founded in her argument for arts and humanities in education. She uses the desires of Soren Kierkegaard to move people from the malaise of ease perpetuated through industrial and technological eras to "awakening" people through making things harder. "It meant communicating to them in such a way that they would become aware of their "personal mode of existence" (Kierkegaard, 1962), their responsibility as individuals in a changing and problematice world" (Greene, 1977, p. 120). Greene further sets "wide-awakeness" through the words of Thoreau's (1963) *Walden*, "The millions are awake enough for physical labor; but only one in a million is awake enough for effective intellectual exertion, only one in a hundred millions to a poetic or divine life. To be awake is to be alive" (pp. 66–67). She notes how the writing and other works of art have been the means to "move people to critical awareness, to a sense of moral agency, and to a conscious engagement with the world" (Greene, 1977, p. 120). Greene's naming of "wide-awakeness" offers what she calls as "concreteness" (p. 121) engaging "sense-making and the understanding of what it is to exist in a world" (p. 124).

For us, to practice hope is to engage in "wide-awakeness" as Greene suggests—being aware of what it means to think and act in higher education and realising how that connects beyond to the local and global communities—by rethinking students, academics, and administrators as public intellectuals. As public intellectuals, we position students, academics, and administrators in a state of "wide-awakeness"—moving from the limited view and actions of neoliberalism and the student as consumer, academic as service provider, and administrator as CEO to students, academics, and administrators willing "to respond to actual problems and real interests, to the requirements of sense-making in a confusing world. It may also involve identification of lacks and insufficiencies in that world—and some conscious effort to repair those lacks, to choose what ought to be" (Greene, 1977, p. 123).

We recognize that our example of rethinking of higher education through the public intellectual is not new (Cushman, 1999; Giroux, 1988, 2004, 2006, 2010; Goodson, 1999; Lynch, 2006). We are inspired by this previous work to help us define our practice of hope through the public intellectual but draw on Said's (1996) framing of the public intellectual as a foundational component to our example of the practice of hope. For Said, a public intellectual is a person who raises questions that may not be welcomed, faces accepted practices and dominant doctrines head on, and resists the influence of corporation—all "wide-awake" actions outside expected neoliberal roles of the higher education student, academic, and administrator and the current context of the university.

Said (1996) builds his idea of the public intellectual on the frames of Benda (1969), Foucault (1980), and Gramsci (1971). Gramsci's (1971) foundational idea that, "all men are intellectuals, one could therefore say: but not all men have in society the function of intellectuals" (p. 9) illustrates how the potential for anyone within society to be an intellectual but not everyone operates as an intellectual. He divides the performing intellectuals into two categories: traditional intellectual and organic intellectual. The traditional intellectual are people in powerful and service-oriented positions like teachers or clergy, continuously performing the same duties as intellectual throughout the years. While the organic intellectual is more active, striving to shift people's views and expand ideas. Benda (1969) on the other hand, believes there is only a small segment of people with the moral ability and appropriate gifts to be intellectuals. This group of intellectuals consistently resists and challenges the status quo in regard to betterment of society, regardless of how it may impact them as individuals. Foucault (1980) identifies the "specific intellectual" as a person with the specific expertise, functioning within this discipline, but able to work beyond that discipline in a multi-disciplinary sense. All of these understandings form how Said (1996) defines the intellectual as "an individual endowed with a faculty for representing, embodying, articulating a message, a view, an attitude, philosophy or opinion to, as well for, a public" (p. 11). He further states,

And this role has an edge to it, and cannot be played without a sense of being someone whose place it is publicly to raise embarrassing questions, to confront orthodoxy and dogma (rather than produce them), to be someone who cannot easily be co-opted by government or corporations, and whose *raison d'être* is to represent all those people and issues that are routinely forgotten or swept under the rug.

(p. 11)

The vocation of the public intellectual is work within the public sphere, articulating the means to equity, recognizing the "contest between a powerful system of interests on the one hand, and on the other, less powerful interests threatened with frustration, silence, incorporation, or extinction by the powerful" (Said, 2002, p 31). Said refers to a "contest" in constructing the role of public intellectual, "The intellectual's role generally dialectically, oppositionally, to uncover and elucidate the contest… ….to challenge and defeat both an imposed silence and the normalized quiet of the unseen power wherever and whenever possible" (p. 31). It should be further noted that Said (1996) recognizes that "no major revolutions in modern history without intellectuals; conversely there has been no major counterrevolutionary movement without intellectuals" (p. 11).

While the public intellectual is situated to disrupt and rethink systems and meta-narratives, she may also be contributing to the creation of the very systems and stories she is trying to counter (Said, 1996). This tension is real and should be recognized by the intellectual as part of how to function in terms of contesting and constructing counter actions and narratives. Another challenge for the public intellectual is the fact that a public intellectual is "actively willing" to engage publicly (Said, 1996, p. 23) and with this choice, exile, misalignment, and marginality are also a possibility. While this may be seen as limiting, engaging as a public intellectual also positions a person with privilege and this exile can be a source of positive action and way to see beyond traditional constructions of an institution. "Exile may be one of the few spaces left in neoliberal societies as democracy is pushed ever farther to the margins where individuals must learn to work together to cultivate a sense of meaningful connection, solidarity, and engaged citizenship that moves beyond an allegiance to narrow interest groups and fragmented, single issue politics" (Giroux, 2016).

What/Who/Where is the Public in the Public Intellectual?

Greene (1986) offers a way for us to think about the public as "public spaces" as where "a better state of things can be imagined; because it is only through the project of a better social order that we can perceive the gaps in what exists and try to transform and repair" (pp. 247–248). This idea of "public spaces" positions the public as active as it is where awareness of what is limiting and unjust lives and change and transformation is imagined. Dewey (1927) notes how the public is a perpetual position of reaching towards the possibilities of the futures. The public becomes the public when a problem arises as individuals and groups come together to figure out how to address the conflict. And while the public is meant to support the power of the state (or nation or commonwealth)—the public is also constructed to disrupt and offer another perspective. Much like Said (1996) situates the public intellectual as the person to question, disrupt, resist, and rethink, Dewey notes how the public has an oppositional capacity to engage in the same manner. Again, the public is an action, a constructed space of movement.

And while the public could be seen as an action, if we consider Dewey (1927), Greene (1986), and Said (1996), the public only exists in contention, when a change is essential, when the world needs to be imagined as otherwise. In this sense, the public for the public intellectual is the audience that is non-existence and only through the provocation of the intellectual, does the public exist.

> Publics, as John Dewey argued, never simply exist; they are always created. Created out of groups of people who are made and mangled by the actions of other people. Capital acts upon labor, subjugating men and women at work, making them miserable at home. Those workers are not yet a public. But when someone says—someone writes—"Workers of the world, unite!," they become a public that is willing and able to act upon its shared situation. It is in the writing of such words, the naming of such names—"Workers of the world" or "We, the People," even "The Problem That Has No Name"—that a public is summoned into being. In the act of writing for a public, intellectuals create the public for which they write.
> (Robin, 2016)

Media and social networking play a part in provocation, in building the public. Said (2002) shares, "I am constantly surprised (and don't know whether to be angry or flattered) when something that I wrote or said in one place turns up with scarcely a delay halfway across the world" (p. 28). In our own work, we experience this same type of movement. Our most recent commentary published in *Teachers College Record* (Iorio & Tanabe, 2015b) "Early Childhood Pushes Up: The Incredible Ridiculousness of the Readiness Chain" focuses on the dominating discourse regarding readiness. While this commentary has been viewed over 2900 times (October 2016) through *Teachers College Record*, it has also been picked up by numerous public blogs (http://ecepolicyworks.com/; http://www.susanohanian.org/; www.dianeravitch.net) and social media (twitter, facebook, pinterest). The movement of the piece from one source *Teachers College Record* to across the electronic public space contributes to how the public is created—mostly out of the control of the author—and in the hands of technology.

Technology, Public, and the Anti-public Intellectual

Technology is very relevant as we write this text as we consider the public being created by the current President of the United States Donald Trump. As President Trump continues to tweet his disagreements, opinions, government decisions, and implied policy directives on Twitter, the immediate access via Twitter is creating another type of public. Trump's tweets become a tool for him to create another public—a public provoked and constructed through the public anti-intellectual. Trump readily identifies as an anti-public intellectual and in this sense, makes determinations without understanding an issue or the implications of a decision or without the input of the people or communities his choice impacts (Cillizza, 2017). In his decision to ban certain news and media from briefings and hand-picking supportive and conservative press, the narrow view of what the public knows is limited by the publication of biased perspectives. During the a speech at the Conservative Political Action Conference, President Trump described journalists as "the enemy of the people" and called for the elimination of the use of anonymous sources (Trump, 2017). By attacking the media, Trump is engaging "a deliberate strategy to undermine public confidence and trust by sowing confusion and uncertainty about what is true" (Simon, 2017). Trump's tweets and restriction of the press give rise to a Trump's public reflective of an autocracy and not a democracy.

Why the Practice of Hope Now More Than Ever?

Klein (2017) reminds us that "US presidency impacts everyone on earth. No one is fully protected from the actions of the world's largest economy, the planet's second-largest emitter of greenhouse gases, and the nation with the world's largest military arsenal" (p. 39). Further,

> It is inconceivable that Trump understands the extent to which the right-wing neoliberalism that fuels his comprehension of the world is exacerbating inequality, sharpening racial divisions through the most repugnant efforts at scapegoating, reprivatizing public rights won over the past half century, destroying public education through a corporatizing of the entire system in a race to the '"bottom line," eclipsing social democracy, increasing the ever-expanding migrations of people, augmenting regional armed conflict, destabilizing national security and raising the specter of fascism that could lead the United States into a world war.
>
> (McLaren, 2016)

This constructs our current condition in the world as imperative for action. As we see Trump as the consequence of neoliberalism, we recognise the "profound emptiness at the heart of the very culture that spawned Donald Trump" (p. 132)—something that has be building over time. This "emptiness" as Klein describes is related to the rise of the branding from mid-1980s, when corporations began to produce brands rather than products, yet another symptom of neoliberalism. This placed the value of a company in "design, innovation, and of course marketing" rather than creating and manufacturing a product (p. 65). The implications created a commitment of corporations to "weightlessness"—"whoever owned the least, had the fewest employees on the payroll, and produced the most powerful images as opposed to things" became the most successful. We have witnessed the rise of "weightlessness" in higher education. We see universities focused on creating the university brand. This has caused large amounts of redundancies across the higher education context with full professors and renowned scholars targeted to cut costs and ensure the "brand" is not challenged. The brand becomes foremost in administration, with little or no discussion or engagement in considering how degree programs will support complex thinking. Rather, the brand becomes about how many customers can we sell our story to in order to bring in as many tuition dollars (students) as possible. As billboards line the highways with marketing slogans of an university brand and academics' inboxes are full of emails from the marketing department on how to better build the brand, the "emptiness" of university culture predominants. This "emptiness" harks back to how Greene (1997) describes the "dark times" and "shadows" shared at the start of this chapter.

As we return to the descriptions of Maxine Greene, we see parallels to Klein's (2017) call to say "yes" and Ayers's (2016) "demand" of the impossible to Greene's (1997) use of "imagination" and movement towards "light". Klein's (2017) "yes" is about resistance—first, understanding "shock politics" and knowing who benefits from this practice (p. 34). And then, telling a different story, a "compelling" story that contends the story of "shock". Ayers (2016) speaks of the "what if?—noting how when the question is taken up by a group, as a collective, it can tell an alternative story, "a powerful tool with the potential to crack open the given world and provide previously unthinkable alternatives" (p. 26). What we know from these scholars and our own experiences in higher education, that now more than ever, graduating students able and willing to contribute as citizens rather than consumers is critical. As Giroux (2016) reminds us, higher education is powerful institution with the ability to address social inequities and lead the process of democracy. Academics need to offer alternative aspects on how to view the world beyond neoliberalism. Administrators must make and support policies that give agency to students and academics to engage with and about the public towards justice. A revolution is needed in order to shift the university from profit-driven decision making to contributing to thoughtful, equity-driven democracy. The positioning of the student, academic, and administrator as public intellectual works to contest the powerful system of neoliberalism in higher education, empowering each to active dialogue, uncover, challenge, resist, and rethink towards equity rather than free market, consumerism, and privatisation, kindling the "light" Greene (1997) describes. Our practice of hope frames how this can begin.

References

Andrews, P. (2010). Hope and the many discourses of education. *Cambridge Journal of Education, 4*(4), 323–326.
Apple, M. (2001). Comparing neo-liberal projects and inequality in education. *Comparative Education, 37*(4), 409–423.
Arendt, H. (1968). *Men in dark times*. New York: Harcourt Brace & Company.
Astin, A. W. (1998). The changing American college student: Thirty-year trends, 1966–1996. *The Review of Higher Education, 21*(2), 115–135.
Ayers, W. (2016). *Demand the impossible*. Chicago: Haymarket Books.
Baik, C., Naylor, R., & Arkoudis, S. (2015). *The first year experience in Australian universities: Findings from two decades, 1994–2014*. Melbourne: Melbourne Centre for the Study of Higher Education.
Benda, J. (1969/2006). *The treason of the intellectuals*. Piscataway, NJ: Transaction Publishers.
Benjamin, A. (1997). *Present hope: Philosophy, architecture, Judaism*. London: Routledge.
Bexley, E., & Arkoudis, J. R. (2013). The motivations, values and future plans of Australian academics. *Higher Education Quarterly, 65*, 385–400.

Billot, J. (2010). The imagined and the real: identifying the tensions for academic identity. *Higher Education Research & Development, 29*(6), 709–721.

Blas Pedreal, M. L. (2015). Hope as a potential transformative power. *The Vermont Connection, 34*(3), 17–22.

Bloch, E. (1995). *The principle of hope* (Vols. 1–3). Cambridge, MA: The MIT Press.

Brown, W. (2015). *Undoing the demos: Neoliberalism's stealth revolution*. New York: Zone Books.

Burns, J. (2016). Where do I fit in? Adrift in neoliberal educational anti-culture. *Teachers College Record*. Retrieved from http://www.tcrecord.org/Content.asp?ContentID=20275.

Comaroff, J. (2011). The end of neoliberalism? *The ANNALS of the American Academy of Political and Social Science, 637*(1), 141–147.

Cillizza, C. (2017). *Donald Trump isn't an intellectual. And he's very proud of that*. Retrieved from https://www.washingtonpost.com/news/the-fix/wp/2017/01/19/the-aggressive-anti-intellectualism-of-donald-trump/?utm_term=.e9a2c02d7d78.

Cote, M., de Peuter, G., & Day, R. (2007). *Utopian pedagogy: Radical experiments against neoliberal globalization*. Toronto: University of Toronto Press.

Cunningham (2016) Production of consumer spaces in the university. *Journal of Marketing for Higher Education, 26*(2), 199–213. https://doi.org/10.1080/08841241.2016.1238023.

Cushman, E. (1999). *Opinion: The public intellectual, service learning, and activist research* (p. 84). General: Service Learning.

Dahlberg, G., & Moss, P. (2005). *Ethics and politics in early childhood education*. London and New York : Routledge Falmer.

Davies, W. (2016). *The limits of neoliberalism: Authority, sovereignty and the logic of competition*. New York: Sage.

Dewey, J. (1927/2012). *The public and its problems*. University Park, Pennsylvania: Penn State Press.

Else, H. (2015). *The rise in teaching only contracts*. Retrieved from https://www.timeshighereducation.com/news/rise-in-teaching-only-contracts/2019008.article.

Foucault, M. (1980). Power/knowledge: Selected interviews and other writings 1972–1977. In C. Gordon (Ed.), pp. 127–28. New York: Panetheon.

Foucault, M. (1987). The ethic of care for the self as a practice of freedom. In J. Bernauer & D. Rasmussen (Eds.), *The final Foucault*. Cambridge: MIT Press.

Foucault, M., Burchell, G., Gordon, C., & Miller, P. P. D. (1991). *The Foucault effect: Studies in governmentality: With two lectures by and an interview with Michel Foucault* (p. 1991). Chicago: University of Chicago Press.

Friedman, M. (1962). *Capitalism and freedom*. Chicago, IL: University of Chicago Press.

Friedman, M. (2005). The promise of vouchers. Retrieved from https://www.wsj.com/articles/SB113374845791113764.

Freire, P. (1972). *Pedagogy of the oppressed*. Harmondsworth: Penguin.

Freire, P. (1978). *Pedagogy in process*. London: Writers and Readers Publishing Cooperative.

Freire, P. (1992). *Pedagogy of hope*. London: Bloomsbury.

Freire, P. (1998). *Pedagogy of freedom*. Lanham, MD: Rowman and Littlefield.

Freire, P. (2007). *Daring to dream*. Boulder, Colorado: Paradigm.

Giroux, H. (1988). *Teachers as intellectuals*. New York: Praeger.

Giroux, H. (2004). Cultural studies, public pedagogy, and the responsibility of intellectuals. *Communication and Critical/Cultural Studies, 1*(1), 59–79.

Giroux, H. (2005). *The terror of neoliberalism: Cultural politics and the promise of democracy*. Boulder Co: Paradigm Publishers.

Giroux, H. (2006). Higher education under siege: Implications for public intellectuals, *Thought & Action*, 63–78.

Giroux, H. (2010). Bare pedagogy and the scourge of neoliberalism: Rethinking higher education as a democratic public sphere. *The Educational Forum, 74*, 184–196.

References

Giroux, H. (2013/2014).Public intellectuals against the neo-liberal university. In N.K. Denzin and M. Giardina (Eds.), *Qualitative inquiry outside the academy* (pp. 35–60). Walnut Creek, CA: Left Coast Press.

Giroux, H. (2016). *Exile as a space of disruption in the academy*. Retrieved from http://www.truth-out.org/opinion/item/34680-exile-as-a-space-of-disruption-in-the-academy).

Goodson, I. (1999). The educational researcher as a public intellectual. *British Educational Research Journal, 25,* 277–297.

Grace, G. (1994). Urban education and the culture of contentment: The politics, culture and economics of inner-city schooling. In N. Stromquist (Ed.), *Education in urban areas: Cross-national dimensions* (pp. 45–59). Westport, CT: Praeger.

Gramsci, A. (1971). *Selections from the prison notebooks*. New York: International Publishers.

Greene, M. (1977). Toward wide-awakeness: An argument for the arts and humanities in education. *Teachers College Record, 79*(1), 119–125.

Greene, M. (1986). In search of a critical pedagogy. *Harvard Educational Review, 56*(4), 427–441.

Greene, M. (1995). *Releasing the imagination: Essays on education, the arts, and social change*. San Francisco: Jossey-Bass.

Greene, M. (1997). Teaching as possibility: A light in dark times. *The Journal of Pedagogy, Pluralism & Practice, 1*(1), 1–11.

Haiven, M. (2014). *Crises of imagination, crises of power: Capitalism, creativity and the commons*. New York, NY: Zed Books.

Halpin, D. (2001). The nature of hope and its significance for education. *British Journal of Educational Studies, 49*(4), 392–410.

Harman, C. (2008). Theorizing neoliberalism. *International Socialism, 117*.

Harper, V. (2014). *Henry A. Giroux: Neoliberalism, democracy and the university as a public sphere*. Retreived from http://www.truth-out.org/opinion/item/23156-henry-a-giroux-neoliberalism-democracy-and-the-university-as-a-public-sphere.

Hardt, M., & Negri, A. (2002). Subterranean passages of thought: Empire's inserts. *Cultural Studies, 16*(2), 201.

Havel, V. (1989). *Letters to Olga*. New York: Henry Holt.

Hope, J. (2017). Make good use of data to retain your students. *Enrollment Management Report, 20,* 1–5. https://doi.org/10.1002/emt.30246.

Iorio, J.M. & Tanabe, C.S. (2015a). A modest proposal re-imagined: Disrupting and rethinking educational decision-making. *Teachers College Record*. Retreived from December 10, 2015, from http://www.tcrecord.org, ID Number: 18828.

Iorio, J.M. & Tanabe, C.S. (2015b). Early childhood finally pushes up: The incredible ridiculousness of the readiness chain. *Teachers College Record*, Date Published: November 13, 2015, from http://www.tcrecord.org, ID Number: 18264.

James, R., Krause, K-L. & Jennings, C. (2010). *The first year experience in Australian universities: Findings from 1994 to 2009*.

Kierkegaard, S. (1962). *The Point of View for My Work as an Author* In B. Nelson (Ed.), (pp. 45--53). New York: Harper Torchbooks.

Klein, N. (2007). *The shock doctrine: The rise of disaster capitalism*. Canada: Random House.

Klein, N. (2017). *No is not enough: Resisting Trump's shock politics and winning the world we need*. Chicago, IL: Haymarket Books.

Larkin, F. (2011). Academic staffing trends: At what cost to teaching and learning excellence? *Insights Blog*. Retrieved from http://www.lhmartininstitute.edu.au/insights-blog/2011/10/65-academic-staffing-trends-at-what-cost-to-teaching-and-learning-excellence.

Lemke, T. (2001). 'The birth of bio-politics': Michel Foucault's lecture at the College de France on neo-liberal governmentality. *Economy and Society, 30*(2), 190–207.

Lynch, K. (2006). Neo-liberalism and marketisation: the implications for higher education. *European Educational Research Journal, 5*(1), 1–17.

Macquarrie, J. (1966). *Principles of Christian theology*. London: SCM Press.

Marginson, S. (2004). Competition and markets in higher education: a "glonacal" analysis. *Policy futures in education, 2*(2), 175–244.
Marginson, S. (2016). *Higher education and the common good.* Melbourne, AU: MUP Academic.
Marginson, S., & Considine, M. (2000). *The enterprise university: governance, strategy, reinvention.* Melbourne: Cambridge University Press.
McLaren, P. (2016). *A message to social studies educators of the US in the coming trump era.* Retrieved from http://www.truth-out.org/opinion/item/38926-a-message-to-social-studies-educators-of-america-in-the-coming-trump-era.
Mirowski, P. (2011). *Science-mart.* Cambridge, MA: Harvard University Press.
Molesworth, M., Scullion, R., & Nixon, E. (Eds.). (2010). *The marketisation of higher education and the student as consumer.* London: Routledge.
Moltmann, J. (1967). *Theology of hope: On the ground and the implications of Christian eschatology.* London: SCM Press.
Monbiot, G. (2016a). *Neoliberalism—The ideology at the root of all of our problems.* Retrieved from https://www.theguardian.com/books/2016/apr/15/neoliberalism-ideology-problem-george-monbiot.
Monbiot, G. (2016b). Retrieved from https://www.theguardian.com/commentisfree/2016/nov/14/neoliberalsim-donald-trump-george-monbiot.
Nelson, K., Kift, S, Clarke, J. (2012). A transition pedagogy for student engagement and first-year learning success and retention, In Solomonides, I, Reid, A., Petocz (Eds.) *Engaging with learning in higher education* (pp. 117–144). Oxfordshire: Libri Publishers.
Pacini-Ketchabaw, V., Nxumalo, F., Kocher, L., Elliot, E., & Sanchez, A. (2015). *Journeys: Reconceptualizing early childhood practices through pedagogical narration.* Canada: University of Toronto Press.
Probert, B. (2013) *Teaching-focused academic appointments in Australian universities: Recognition, specialisation, or stratification?* Office for Learning and Teaching Discussion Paper Series (pp. 1–46).
Probert, B. (2014) *Why scholarship matters in higher education.* Office for Learning and Teaching Discussion Paper Series (pp. 1–28).
Robertson, C. (2016). *Millions on election day make a different decision: Not voting.* Retrieved from https://www.nytimes.com/2016/11/09/us/politics/voter-turnout.html.
Rowland, J. & Rawolle, S. (2013). Neoliberalism is not a theory of everything: A Bourdieuian analysis of illusio in educational research. *Critical Studies in Education, 54*(3), 260–272. (http://dx.doi.org/10.1080/17508487.2013.830631.
Robin, C. (2016). *How intellectuals create a public.* Retrieved from (http://www.chronicle.com/article/How-Intellectuals-Create-a/234984)
Said, E. (1996). *Representations of the intellectual: the 1993 Reith Lectures.* London, UK: Vintage Books.
Said, E. W. (2002) The public role of writers and intellectuals. In H Small (Ed.) *The public intellectual.* Malden, MA: Blackwell Publishers Ltd.
Saunders, D. (2011a). *Students as customers: The influence of neoliberal ideology and free-market logic on entering first-year college students.* Amherst, MA: University of Massachusetts.
Saunders, D. (2011b). Neoliberal ideology and public higher education in the United States. *Journal for Critical Education Policy Studies, 8*(1), 41–77.
Simon, J. (2017). *Trump is damaging press freedom in the U.S. and abroad.* Retrieved from https://www.nytimes.com/2017/02/25/opinion/trump-is-damaging-press-freedom-in-the-us-and-abroad.html?action=click&contentCollection=Politics&module=RelatedCoverage&region=Marginalia&pgtype=article).
Tarnoff, B. (2016). *Neoliberalism turned our world into a business. And there are two big winners.* Retrieved from https://www.theguardian.com/us-news/2016/dec/13/donald-trump-silicon-valley-leaders-neoliberalism-administration).
Thomas, L. (2002). Student retention in higher education: the role of institutional habitus. *Journal Of Education Policy, 17* (4).

References

Thoreau, H. D. (1963). *The variorum Walden*. New York: Washington Square Press.
Trump, D. (2017). *Full transcript: President Trump's CPAC speech*. Retrieved from https://www.vox.com/policy-and-politics/2017/2/24/14726584/transcript-donald-trump-cpac-speech.
Webb, D. (2010). Paulo Freire and 'the need for kind of education in hope. *Cambridge Journal of Education, 40*(4), 327–339.
West, C. (2016). *Goodbye, American neoliberalism. A new era is here*. Retrieved from https://www.theguardian.com/commentisfree/2016/nov/17/american-neoliberalism-cornel-west-2016-election).
Zepke, N. (2014). Student engagement research in higher education: questioning an academic orthodoxy. *Teaching in Higher Education, 19*(6), 697–708.

Chapter 3
Student as Public Intellectual

> *We grant this neoliberal order in the university will be somewhat dear, and therefore very proper for students, who as they have already been commodified by society, easily fall into the view of students as consumers.*
>
> *The student as consumer will be in season throughout the year, more evident in scales of customer satisfaction and driven to higher education by state-of-the-art workout facilities, free wi-fi, and good coffee. It is not improbable that some scrupulous people might be apt to censure such a practice of student is consumer (although indeed very unjustly) as a little bordering upon cruelty; which, we confess, hath always been with us the strongest objection against any project, how well soever intended. But in order to justify the student as consumer, we use the rhetoric of "tangible and marketable skills" (Brulé, 2004, p. 253) as fiscal gain feeds appropriately into the ego of the student and amplifies the commitment of the consumer.*
>
> **The absurd:** *...and therefore very proper for students, who as they have already been commodified by society, easily fall into the view of students as consumers.*

In a recent Australian first-year early childhood teacher education course focused on the study of development, students shared negative feedback stating that they were not taught developmental psychology within the structure of the course. This course was structured to foreground Aboriginal epistemologies and pedagogies as well as alternative conceptions of development in order to disrupt traditional early childhood practices steeped in Western knowledge and ideals. This student feedback implied that there is assumption that the Western dominant paradigm is the only way to understand how to teach young children. For these students, teaching is not seen as a political practice and therefore does not relate to oppression and racism. These implications indicate the ease in which students demand and how the product (in this case, the degree) is more critical than any type of deep and thoughtful engagement with a practice.

The student as consumer (Brulé, 2004; Edmundson, 1997; Maringe, 2010; Molesworth, Scullion, & Nixon, 2010; Molesworth, Nixon, & Scullion 2009; Newson 2004; Saunders, 2011) is over four decades in the making and an outgrowth of the neoliberal context in the university. When the student is the consumer, satisfaction of the consumer dominates the relationship between student and academic. Choices within curriculum and practice made by the faculty and often governed by what might give the student the most satisfaction. Keep in mind, this satisfaction is defined by the student and not the academic, so this satisfaction is rooted in how to get the most value for your money rather than the rigor and challenge of learning something new.

Students use this consumer model as a way to affirm their rights as students. It should be noted that these "rights" are reflective of the customer and are rooted in satisfaction as defined by the student. Brulé (2004), Course Director in the Department of Equity Studies, York University, offers an example of how a student professes his rights as consumer when asked to submit a rough draft of an essay for a Women's studies course,

> How come I'm being asked to provide drafts of my essay? Are they accusing me of plagiarism? I would never be treated like this in the private sector. I am a consumer and I have a right to be treated and served in a way that gives me what I am here for—an education. There is no way this would happen in the business world. I have rights as a consumer and I'm thinking of getting a lawyer.
>
> (p. 256)

Brulé then shares,

> This student's comments are particularly insightful. Rather than following the process outlined in the University's rules governing suspected cases of plagiarism and speaking directly with the instructor, he sees his rights as a consumer superseding any notion of academic honesty or integrity. In doing so, he reduces the social relations of learning and teaching to particular notions of "customer service," which, ironically, do not constitute substantiating whether he has done the work himself or not. Not only does he use consumer relations as a means to assert his rights as a student but he also compares the university to a business and appeals to the judicial system as a way to enforce what he sees as his consumer rights. Educational accountability in this context is reduced to whether services have been rendered or not.
>
> (p. 256)

This example illustrates how student rights, framed by the view of the student as consumer, position satisfaction as the ultimate goal in the neoliberal model of the university. Students as consumers overpower any educational goal beyond student satisfaction. When the customer service model defines satisfaction, measurable outcomes likes marks or grades, speed of an email response, and amount of time spent outside of a class on readings and related activities become the defining descriptions of learning and teaching. Beyond this, the university experience is less about engaging with the public good, democracy, and change and more focused on individual contentment.

Students as consumers are positioned to support any type of money making initiative and are a tool within the system focused on return on investment. Examples of how students are consumers in the university are quite telling. Recreation and state-of-the-art workout facilities are the first stop on a campus tour when trying to entice students to attend the university. Hacker and Dreifus (2010) describe Kenyon College's fitness center, "a $70 million palace of a gym, complete with a twenty-lane swimming pool, indoor tennis and squash courts, an all-weather running track, Wi-Fi Internet, and two hundred pieces of exercise equipment" (p. 114). In this sense, the experience is being sold to the students; "these commodified experiences range from athletics events to gym memberships to the central service provided: education, which more explicitly bears the markings of the commodity form" (Cunningham, 2016, p. 201).

Academically in the neoliberal university, the student experience in the classroom is often lead by part-time sessionals or adjuncts as more than 50% of all college appointments are held by part-time staff/faculty (Hoeller, 2014). And these part-time staff have much less privilege than full-time continuing contract or tenure-track positions as they receive less pay, little benefits, no guarantee of work, and sometimes, not even an office (Hoeller, 2014). Their contracts have little time for actually meeting with students outside of class or a dedicated space (office) for meeting with students. With little or no funding for the part-time sessionals or adjuncts to understand or engage with the tenets of the overall program or course, teaching is often surface with no relation to the rest of the program/course.

The expansion of online and blended learning modes in order to accelerate the speed of obtaining a degree with the intent of placating the market have little regard for developing the intellectual and critical thought of students (Cunningham, 2016). Unit guides and syllabi are no longer working documents responsive to students' ideas, rather they are fixed and meant to be pre-packaged, never taking into account who the student is or what they might bring to the unit/class/university (Saunders, 2011). Students decide to enrol in a course/program based on how accessible it is through technology rather than the academic subject.

Courses and programs are driven by distinctly profitable skills and workforce development is paramount to the purpose of higher education. Knowledge that relates to immediate fiscal gain is prioritized while social knowledge like humanities is secondary and often implied as worthless (Blackmore, 1997; Brulé, 2004). Yet, the humanities provide the roadmap, the direction, for the unique potential of the human future. The humanities work toward diversity, full, and unique expression. And it is in this diversity that we understand the breadth and depth of what it means to be human.

The student as consumer is "de-sexed, de-raced, de-classed"—anonymous—assumed to be able to make rational economic decisions only regarding employment (Brulé, 2004, p. 255) as "neoliberalism instills consumerist and career connotations to higher education" (Cunningham, 2016, p. 201). Anything outside this one glaring purpose of workforce development is considered futile. This becomes evident as working towards equity and social justice is seen as costly and irrelevant, "a luxury only the privileged can afford" (p. 255) in realm of the neoliberal university (Ibbitson, 2000). This presents another tension as neoliberalism may open access to universities for low-income and non-traditional students, but only in a very limited sense as these students' lack of privilege narrows how they engage with learning with economic benefit as the only purpose. An example of this is the three-year education-related bachelor degrees, meeting the need of the student as consumer—quick and easy. Yet, these degrees limit the job trajectory at a certain level within the field. While the degree may be cost effective and meet the needs of the consumer, it is perpetuating the status quo—keeping those low-income and non-traditional students in the their place of less privilege and power.

And while the student as a consumer may seem to place most of the power in the higher education context to the student, student as consumer is also quite limiting to the student. The neoliberal order within the university is constructed to only allow the student to act as consumer (Cunningham, 2016). "Ultimately, the spatial production of consumer spaces in the university operates as a form of control; spaces are produced to produce individuals who are complicit with the current economic system" (p. 208). A strong example of this is the reliance on the technology of a computer or mobile phone even within the face-to-face teaching experience. Often described as blended learning, students are required to log a certain amount of hours in the university online platform along with using laptops or handheld technology to participate in in-class polls, twitter feeds, or live blogging. This is further supported when policies regarding class structures required a certain amount of a class/unit be delivered through an online mode. The university deems the use of technology as an obligation to be a student, rather than a necessity to learn (Cunningham, 2016). In some communities where non-traditional and low-income students matriculate, these university obligations exist, foregrounding neoliberalism over the true understanding of the community the university is serving.

This regulation of the student as consumer is further evident through student codes of conduct. Through the use of "managerial technologies" (Griffith & Smith, 2014) policies regarding management of risk and space as well as surveillance of students (in this case, students are viewed as incapable and not competent by the university) "are used to align students' non-academic behaviour with a corporate understanding of students as clients" (Brulé, 2015). Any type of activism, individual or in association with a campus club, is now often penalised in the name of the "language of civility and inclusiveness" reframing "students' social citizenship rights as a matter of individual choice and reasonableness, thereby promoting their interests as clients while undermining the most basic social rights of others" (p. 160). This manipulation of students ensures the actions of the student as consumer under the guise of supposed advocacy and activism. Students are essentially depoliticized, creating a significant cog in the neoliberal machine and ensuring the depoliticization of higher education (Cunningham, 2016; Pusey, 2016; Sealey-Huggins & Pusey, 2013) and perpetuation of neoliberalism.

Returning to Story of the Development Course

At the start of this chapter, we shared a story of undergraduate early childhood students in an Australian university complaining about a development class. For us, these students were acting as consumers, ensuring their rights as students through the consumer model. While their actions reflected a customer mentality, these same students articulated another version of how they see themselves as students, almost resisting the students as consumer view. As a visiting scholar to this university, Clif led a lecture and discussion.

The following questions were asked to these same students:

> If you could custom build your university education, what would it look like?
>
> What is important to you about a university education?
>
> What do you want out of your university education?
>
> What do you feel the university needs to give you?
>
> What outcome do you expect as a result of going to the university?
>
> What return on investment do you require from the time, energy and capital you have invested in your university educational experience?.

(October 2015)

The students created this list in response to the questions:

> ….to be challenged to think outside of the box;
>
> ….to have meaningful experiences and engagement;
>
> ….to be challenged to think critically;
>
> ….to be motivated;
>
> ….to be a better self;
>
> ….to have more input into the curriculum;
>
> ….to be equipped with knowledge that will help me in the field;
>
> ….to build my self confidence;
>
> ….to have better relationships with staff; and
>
> ….to be in a space where I am not afraid to make mistakes.

(October 2015)

There is an evident tension between what these students share on this list and the view of the student as consumer. How can there be such a difference between what these undergraduates expect and demand as customers with how they imagine a university experience should be? Is there an implied understanding that the university contributes to the public good? Could this gap between how students act as consumers and the possibility of higher education as a institute contributing to democracy be the disconnection needed to disrupt the student as consumer?

Disrupting the Absurd: Rethinking the Student as Public Intellectual

In response to the absurd neoliberal view of the student as consumer, we rethink the student as public intellectual. This view supports "wide-awakeness" as Greene's (1995) imagines, fostering student "awareness of what it is to be in the world" (p. 35). This shift in viewing the student recasts the university as a place "reflective of contemporary ideologies that seek to recast education as a force of intellectual empowerment outside the realm of pure social mobility" (Cunningham, 2016, p. 211). These become "humanized" spaces (Davies & Niemann, 2002) where both learning and social interactions pay attention to matters of equity, aware of neoliberal structures in higher education and beyond, and forming supportive and active collectives that resist, challenge, and rethink. This aligns with Said's (1996) construct of the public intellectual and is realised as students trouble the expected, disrupt the for granted, and confront the presence of market throughout their college experience.

When students are re-positioned as public intellectuals, students are situated to be "wide-awake" (Greene, 1995) and recognize their social responsibility to act as agents of change, as advocates and in some cases, activists, challenging assumptions and power structures that oppress the university and their communities (both locally and globally). Students are no longer seen as passive, "Thus, communities are not seen as composed of passive receptacles into which "expert" knowledge might be poured, but of active living human subjects, possessed of ways of seeing, speaking, thinking, acting, and imagining" (Cote, de Peuter, & Day, 2007, p. 322). For students to act as public intellectuals, there must be opportunities for students to problematize and contest knowledge, engage in complex conversations about how local and global issues could be addressed, while contributing their own ideas and experiences to understanding how the historical, political, social, and economical all add layers to the present daily life (Giroux, 2013). This contributes to repositioning higher education as a "democratic public sphere" providing "students with modes of individual and social agency that enable them to be both engaged citizens and active participants in the struggle for global democracy" (Giroux, 2006, p. 66).

And if we go back to the list the students shared of what they wanted from their university experience, the connection between what the students desire and how students could be constructed as public intellectuals is clear.

Students as Public Intellectuals	Students' list of what they want from their university experience
Students are situated to recognize their social responsibility to act as agents of change, as advocates and in some cases, activists	– to be motivated – to be a better self – to have meaningful experiences and engagement
Students challenge assumptions and power structures that oppress the university and their communities (both locally and globally)	– to be challenged to think critically – to have better relationships with staff
Students are no longer seen as passive—students problematize and contest knowledge, engage in complex conversations about how local and global issues could be addressed, while contributing their own ideas and experiences to understanding	– to have more input into the curriculum – to be challenged to think outside of the box – to be in a space where I am not afraid to make mistakes

The connections indicated in the above table regarding student expectations of university and the possibility of student acting as public intellectual offer a guide in constructing higher education. For example, when students are situated to recognize their social responsibility to act as agents of change, as advocates and in some cases, activists, students are motivated and engage in meaningful experiences towards an active, better self, aware and contributing to the public good. In another instance, students are no longer seen as passive—students problematize and contest knowledge, engage in complex conversations about how local and global issues could be addressed, while contributing their own ideas and experiences to understanding. This supports students to have more input into the curriculum, be challenged to think outside of the box, and to be in a space where they are not afraid to make mistakes.

If we consider the desires of the students in collaboration with the view of the students as public intellectuals, we have a foundation to creating university experiences that contemplate what might be imagined in university setting. Imagination in this sense "gives us the power to expand our vision of reality, to open and vary our perspectives, to achieve empathy with other human beings" (Greene, 2001, p. 29) and create spaces in higher education for students to think, wonder, and act towards the public good. The following stories offer examples of the capacity of imagination when students are positioned as public intellectuals.

Story 1: Early Childhood at University of Hawai'i-West Oahu

The early childhood undergraduate course at University of Hawai'i-West Oahu (United States) is a strong example of how students can be positioned as public intellectuals. This program serves students in remote areas across Hawai'i that are working as practitioners in the field and is completely online. This choice is reflective of the population being served, as without online access, these students could not attend university. When this degree program started in 2007, it was the first access this specific group of students had to receiving an undergraduate degree in early childhood. Inspiring teachers as agents of change is the purpose of the early childhood program. Through this identity, the students are called to critique practice from theoretical and cultural perspectives, interrogate power within the workplace and community, and embrace advocacy so that teacher professionalism evolves as society changes (Adler & Iorio, 2015). While this early childhood program uses the phrase agent of change, we believe this is akin to student as public intellectual as the expectations of the agent of change include questioning, disrupting, and resisting, much like what Said (1996) suggests as public intellectual.

Using both the supplied university online platform, in particular, the discussion board tool, and blogger.com, the students learn how to create questions without answers in the first few weeks of each course. This practice is revisited at the beginning of every class in the program so students are constantly developing the skill of being able to ask questions that confront assumptions and disrupt dogmas in the field. Students' interpretations of their experiences in relationship to the readings and their blogging are central to how each class is delivered, truly creating a "humanized" space to consider themselves and the students and families they will collaborate with as teachers. Two students share through their discussion board and blog postings how this impacts their thinking and understanding of how to work as agents of change,

> ....When we stop to analyze or critique something that is when we use our minds and develop our answers to what we believe in. We cannot always accept everything everyone says because to them, it means something and have created that thought because of an experience, and to say you agree but not look into the situation, you may never know what really is out there. Although professors are the ones that may know a lot of factual information on the topic of teaching, asking questions and wondering why something is the way it is allows you to have an understanding of why it is what it is instead of just accepting what they say without question because the professor may or may not be right depending on the situation.
>
> (Adler & Iorio, 2012, p. 244)
>
> ....To be true advocates in the field of ECE, we all need look into ourselves and not be "sold" into one idea because it came from research or a textbook. Besides the universal ECE shortcomings (wages, respect, gender equity) there are opportunities within our programs to advocate for or against something.
>
> (Adler & Iorio, 2013, p. 133)

Through each posting, students begin to imagine what can be in enacted in early childhood education. Learning about and engaging with critical theory is part of the process as this empowers students to see beyond the narrow possibilities of the technical methods in early childhood education (for example, how to teach literacy or math) and begin to work as advocates for the children, families, and communities where they work. Reading the grand narratives of the field builds the foundation needed for the students to engage critical theory and debate alternative paradigms. For example, one student shares how she is challenging the accepted use of tests and standards in the early childhood classroom,

> Tests and standards hold too much weight in our schools. In fact, they are more important than the well-being of the child. What kind of logic is this? I don't understand why, when there is evidence to suggest otherwise and examples in other countries, parents and educators still insist on the earlier the better. I love Elkind's (1981/1988/2001) phrase "an assault on childhood". We are forcing our future generation to grow up too fast in a system that leads them to feel like they are failures. Imagine a future with no imagination, no creativity and little social skills. What kind of world are we creating?
>
> (Adler & Iorio, 2015, p. 298)

The purpose of this program as inspiring teachers as agents of change develops into the capstone project where students develop and implement an action research project in the classroom where they work. Part of this process is completing 120 hours working in a classroom outside of their own room, using the experience as a mirror on their own teaching practices. Seeing something different, new, otherwise, disrupts what they know in their everyday pedagogies, offering another way to see how they may listen, respond, and engage in the classroom. Students also build a collaborative relationship with a teacher outside of their working setting. This collaboration is a powerful means of support to the student—first, as an undergraduate student and later, as a colleague in the field. This understanding of the important connection between the student and field is reflective of how we see research and practice as a critical part of engaging as an agent of change. This is the beginning of building a collective group of voices able to work towards change and rethinking with the intention of equity for children, families, and communities.

The action research projects include thinking about change in the classroom, often fueled by social justice, personal experience, and awareness of the community. Understanding place, the inclusion of Native Hawaiian pedagogies and epistemologies, and alignment between teacher actions and beliefs are just a few of the topics implemented through the capstone project. For instance, the question, "Will openness in teaching and learning help empower children's learning experiences?" guided one student to videoing her teaching and realising how she was not practicing her belief. Instead control and manipulation drove her practice,

> During the time of my research project, I think that it may have been difficult for the adults within the classroom environment to understand what my research project was about because my observations saw just the opposite of openness. Many of us as teachers and adults may think that we are providing rich learning experiences. But how can we define those experiences as rich when we are the one's controlling the learning taking place? I speak from personal experience. I thought that I was fair and open as a teacher. But when I heard and saw myself on video for the first time I was pleasantly awakened. I saw myself trying to control the learning that was already taking place. There was no need for me to control the outcome of the activity, or achieving the objective. I remember the feelings of frustration that I felt at the time. Why? I ask myself. For the first time, I realized that I needed to let go of my urge to control the learning that was evolving right in front of me. For that very reason, I purposely placed sentences and words camouflaged within my piece. We as teachers and learners may believe that we are providing the best experiences for our children, but are we?
>
> (Shanda, interview with Iorio, 2010)

Rethinking her practice in order to ensure her beliefs as teacher were implemented in her practice became the change in her action research project.

This experience further constructs the students' identity as teacher as agent of change, moving beyond the university and into the community. One student moved her work advocacy into her classroom as well as engaging with at-risk youth creating graffiti. As an agent of change, this teacher worked side-by-side with these students, learning the art of graffiti, with the intent of changing the community perception of this art. She documented the work in her Masters project using autobiography and ethnography illustrate how change happens through the disruption of assumptions. She asks her readers "to take a stand against the power structures that de-humanizes us by looking within and asking yourself, "Why do I want to teach?" The movement starts with you." These words are powerful as this teacher is an agent of change/public intellectual with how she "calls for change not only in herself but also in the people and community around her" (Adler & Iorio, 2015, p. 304).

Being a public intellectual is about moving beyond the walls of the university, disrupting what is known, resisting what is accepted, finding what might be otherwise. As the view of students as consumers is shifted to students as public intellectuals, students can engage beyond the university walls. We see this through the program at University of Hawai'i-West Oahu as students are seen as agents of changes from the start of their course. The faculty support the students to think through this process, offering ways to engage as agents of change first in their coursework and then in their practice through action research.

Story 2: Early Childhood at Victoria University

During the first year of the early childhood/primary program at Victoria University (Australia), undergraduate students engage in two units and a placement, taught together in a seminar-style manner. The content of these units is focused on students as public intellectuals, in particular, respectfully foregrounding Aboriginal Worldviews through play-based pedagogies while completing placement in *Engaging with Place,* a playgroup program for families and children (infant to 6-years-old) available for free to communities throughout the university catchment area. Teaching with complexity is central to the placement and coursework. Students work with three concepts—learning to be affected (Latour, 2004); place-thought (Watts, 2013); and pastpresent (King, 2004) with the intent of the students developing an understanding of what it means to live in post-colonial Australia. These students work in small groups at each site with a mentor teacher, enacting their responsibilities as teachers while inclusively ensuring Aboriginal Worldviews and perspectives are part of learning, teaching, and collaborating with young children and families.

Aboriginal stories and materials (sourced from the local place where the service is situated) are primary parts of *Engaging with the Place.* This choice forefronts Aboriginal epistemologies to pedagogy; this choice places Aboriginal Worldviews as the starting point. As children, families, and teachers name the country, animals, and materials where their *Engaging with Place* is located, the same practices are part of the learning at university. Each week the students think with place, understanding where the university is situated is a place of significance for local Aboriginal people. Place-thought walks, weekly writing, and class discussions all contribute to the space created to engage as public intellectuals. The coursework and placement work together as acts of decolonisation. Academics working in these classes and mentor teachers leading *Engaging with Place* constantly review the activities of the class and placement, ensuring the work is not tokenistic or domesticated. Rather, the academics consider how teaching is always political and how to ethically engage authentically with local place, thinking *with* (rather than about).

Through this experience of the classes and the placement, these first-year students find ways to act as public intellectuals beyond the university. For example, as the refugee crisis for women and children became more prominent, students from the first year joined local activist groups to ensure the rights of these women and children were heard by participating in peaceful, public rallies. The first-year experience empowers students as it illustrates concretely the ways in which a student might act as a public intellectual. It shows students how to question assumptions and disrupt the Western-driven expectations in early childhood in order to create early childhood experiences that respond to post-colonial Australia. Students then move to act independent of the university, to contribute and further democracy where the students live and work.

Description 3: Activist Educators Engaging Listening, Dialogue, and Action

Quintero and Rummel (2003) engage as "activist educators" in their work with undergraduate and graduate students becoming teachers. As they introduce education to these students, they aim to

> ....help our students critically "read" what they are learning in and out of school. We want them to integrate knowledge from social sciences and humanities and to begin to develop their own beliefs about and metaphors for education and social change as well as to analyse those that have been developed by others.
>
> (p. 12)

Steeped in understanding of the current and future local and global communities and issues related to power, globalisation, inequities, and interdependence, a focus on "integrating historical knowledge with humanities, drawing upon wisdom in the fine arts" (p. 13) informs a their framework of teaching reflective of viewing students as public intellectuals. Interdisciplinary and engaging with imagination and metaphor, students are expected to engage in activism and diversity through relevant stories across the field internationally.

Quintero and Rummel (2003) offer a problem-posing framework for engaging their students using Listening, Dialogue, and Action. Listening includes self-reflection connecting personal stories and class/unit content. Dialogue includes discussions with peers, colleagues, and people or groups beyond the university context. Action includes implementing projects that engage and/or rethink practices or investigating ideas, materials, or resources from a cross-cultural perspective, understanding and critically thinking about assumptions, limitations, benefits, and different ways of knowing. A strong example of this is Quintero's (2015) work with family literacy projects and how this informs the teaching and acting with her students.

Quintero begins discussing family literacy in her undergraduate class by provoking her students to think about experiences where they were not able to understand what a person was communicating to them. She suggests it could be a different language, dialect, or discourse, but unfamiliarity was the common factor for not being able to understand. Through writing, students' stories become the text for the class/unit discussion—and the provocation for constructing questions about language, culture, and communication—questions that open debate and dialogue for the students (Quintero, 2015).

Students' stories are also how a space is created for listening. Quintero shares her own experiences, stories, and research in these moments, stories about her research with Latino and Hmong families in Texas and Minnesota (USA). Trust and reciprocal relationships are a critical part of this classroom work as Quintero trusts her students with her stories and the students trust Quintero with their stories (Quintero, 2009). This collaborative setting is set when Quintero shares her own learning in the process, talking about family literacy and how these projects are how families are empowered through participation—where the politics of literacy are unpacked and families' stories are valued.

Dialogue is further engaged as Quintero challenges students to think about expected classroom literacy practices differing from family literacy experiences. Studying the work of educator and activist Paulo Freire together in the classroom offers another opportunity for dialogue as students consider the aim of literacy from his perspective and then in terms of the family literacy projects. Much of the dialogue becomes the fodder for action—actions that are possible for the students to move beyond the limitations and sterility of the university classroom to acting as public intellectuals aware of how teaching is always political and needs to be ethical.

Proposed actions come out of listening and dialogue. Students engage with families in the community through interviews focused on family interactions with young children. In these experiences, interactions are defined by the families and could be anything—cooking, storytelling, camping, eating together—and are the data informing the students to think about literacy beyond expected teaching practices. Consideration of what the "roots" of literacy might be in these interactions becomes the source of rethinking understandings of literacy, connecting to listening and dialogue activities as well as the personal stories of the students. What Quintero has done in her teaching is offered multiple entry points into students engaging as public intellectuals but what is critical to her practice is that Quintero and Rummel's framework is underpinned by the belief that students are capable of being public intellectuals.

In more recent work reflective of 2017 immigration policies lead by the presidential executive order, Quintero working as a teacher educator in Southern California implements listening, dialogue, and action as part of her university classroom. Again, working from the foundational understanding of students as public intellectuals, Quintero listens to the stories of her students as more than half of her students are first generation college students with a large percentage of them from families and communities of migrant farmworkers in California (Callaway-Cole & Quintero, 2017). These student teachers watched local families frightened to bring their children to preschool as the fear of deportation before the end of the school day, leaving their children alone, with no one to pick them up or care for them after school. These real stories collected by the student teachers are extremely relevant to the present state of immigration policy. The following story is part of the in-class dialogue, made visible through the practice of listening by the university student in a local preschool classroom,

> The children sat on the rug for large circle. The teacher asked the children about their upcoming graduation celebration from preschool into kindergarten. She told them that their families are invited, and how she was looking forward to sharing the day with them. A side conversation began among three children. One child said that both of her parents, sister, and grandma were coming to the celebration. Another, Ana, said that only her mom was coming, because her dad was in jail. The third child said out loud, "The police got Ana's dad, teacher, he's not coming!" Ana immediately responded, "No! La migra took my dad. I'm leaving soon to be with my dad. Mom said."

> Later, a group of four boys were working with the magnetic blocks and constructed a large neighborhood. Along with the blocks, they also included train tracks, people figurines, and cars. As I approached them to listen to what they were acting out, I heard one child say, "Para ahi!" as he chased and held one police officer figurine. He also shouted, "Soy la

Description 3: Activist Educators Engaging Listening, Dialogue, and Action   47

migra, te voy a atrapar!" As he caught the figurine that was running away, he said, *"Te atrape, ya te vas para Mexico"*

(Callaway-Cole & Quintero, 2017)

For Quintero, these stories gathered through listening and provocations for dialogue are also the impetus for action. These students as public intellectuals see the power of rethinking their role as teacher, disrupting the expected practice of only working within the early childhood classroom walls, the students situate their teaching as connected to the families and communities. Actions ensue by the student teachers collaboratively with the families. For example, neighborhood walks are organised by families, university students, and teachers to ensure security for children and families during the now daily Immigration and Customs Enforcement pickups. In another instance, these university students provided access to immigrant rights through organising the distribution of the Immigrant Rights Legal Resource Center's "Red Card" for all families impacted.

Disrupting the Absurd: Rethinking Structures and Policies to Support Students as Public Intellectuals

The programs shared in the three stories positioning students "wide-awake" (Greene, 1995) as public intellectuals. We see this at the University of Hawai'i-West Oahu as students are viewed as agents of change. This view of the student aligns with the content, assessments, and activities within each class as well as how the program is delivered. At Victoria University, we see how strong connections between content, placement, and the technical structures of a class can support students as public intellectuals. Through the simple framework of listening, dialogue, and action, we see how a class/unit can be structured to offer a variety of different means of access to how a student can be viewed and engage as a public intellectual within the university setting and beyond.

Ways to begin viewing academics as public intellectuals

1. *Rethinking online programs*

Relevant Policies and Structures: Online Learning, Blended Learning
Often, online and blended programs are created with intention of the student as consumer—flexibility, accessibility, and quick time frame, mostly technical ideas, frame how a program is constructed and delivered. In some instances, administrators have offered monetary incentives to put more classes online. In one university, academics were paid $2000 to put a class all online. What should be noted though is that being all online essentially means that the class

> could stand alone and allow for anyone to teach the class. With this as the purpose then the technical becomes about the ease to transfer the class to any person that teaches the class—academic, adjunct, sessional, graduate student. How does an academic design a class that anyone can teach? The technical is at the foundation of the class so academics then rely on simple versions of the content and tools fostering surveillance (like quizzes, tests, and checklists) rather than anything that would engage in the complexity of a subject. By rethinking the purpose of an online course by first articulating the conceptual of a class, then the pedagogical, and finally the technical, changes how a class is imagined and delivered.

The University of Hawai'i-West Oahu early childhood program, the overall purpose of the program is to inspire teachers as agents of change (conceptual). With this in mind, the use of blogger (technical) becomes the space for questioning assumptions, debate, and resistance (pedagogical). This influences how the online environment is imagined and implemented. Thinking in terms of the conceptual and pedagogical first offers a way to rethink the technical. In the case presented, the blogger tool is the technical and without the conceptual and the pedagogical, it becomes a flat space, a space without contention. With the conceptual and pedagogical informing the technical, blogger becomes an active place, a place where the contention is made public and this contention is the provocation for questioning, disrupting, resisting, and rethinking.

Questions to consider:

1. What is the purpose of the online and/or blended program?
2. What concepts underpin the overall program? What are the concepts that underpin each unit/class in the program?
3. What pedagogy can deliver the concepts of the overall program? What pedagogy can deliver the concepts of each unit/class in the program?
4. What technical components are necessary to teach the underpinning concepts through the appropriate pedagogy in the overall program? What technical components are necessary to teach the underpinning concepts and through the appropriate pedagogy in each unit/class?

Possible actions:

1. Review online and/or blended course offerings (university-wide, college-wide and/or discipline-specific) and articulate the purpose of these offerings as well as the conceptual, pedagogical, and technical aspects of each offering.
2. Create and implement a project to rethink any offering where the conceptual, pedagogical and/or technical cannot be clearly articulated.
3. Begin with one specific program for review and then rethinking.
4. Create each new offering by first articulating the conceptual. Implement the pedagogical and technical based on the conceptual.

2. Rethinking class structures, content, placements

Relevant Policies and Structures: Timetabling, Class Size, Use of Space/Facilities, Placement Experience, Content/Academic Freedom

Traditional university classes are often lectures with discussions/tutorials. Spaces for discussion, debate, and disagreement are often limited by the number of students in a lecture (sometimes even over 200 students) and discussion/tutorials (most at least 25 students). Often driven by space limitations and cost, this becomes more about ticking the boxes and less about how spaces are created for the student to engage as public intellectual.

Rethinking policies that limit space and determine class size could support the use of small class seminars, workshops, or online environments as places for students to move beyond the simple and often surface understandings of a field. Time and activities engaging beyond simplistic and disconnected concepts support students complexifying their fields through deep engagement with the subject.

Along with rethinking class structures is considering the content students engage with through a class. The inclusion of a framework like listening, dialogue, and action (Quintero & Rummel, 2003) within classes supports the connection between content, personal stories, debate, and action. This connection positions students to rethink and wonder within the university setting while at the same time, engaging beyond into the community. Further, a supportive framework like listening, dialogue, and action creates a community of learners, building a safe space for students to engage with the process of learning including being uncomfortable and uncertain with some content and pedagogies.

Questions to consider:

1. What are the policies and structures that construct the technical (class size, length of meeting, etc.) within a program? In what ways can these policies be flexible or re-imagined in order to support students to engage as public intellectuals?
2. Are classes/units structured to build a community of learners, safe to question, wonder, and be uncomfortable together? Is there a framework (like listening, dialogue, act) that might support a community of learners in a class/unit?
3. Are classes/units structured to create space for debate and dialogue? What needs to change in order to create classes/units for debate and dialogue?
4. What content is taught in a program or class/unit? Does the content only reflect the technical of a discipline? Are there possibilities of critique and uncertainty in the content? Does the content support students to engage as public intellectuals? What content is needed to challenge students to question assumptions, rethink, and act in the local and global communities?

Possible actions:

1. Bring together the teaching team, program head, and students to review the policies and structures governing the technical perspectives in a program. If there is a commitment to engaging students as public intellectuals, discuss if these technical policies and structures support this engagement.
2. Bring together the teaching team, program head, and students to rethink and rewrite any technical policies and structures that limit the potential of students engaging as public intellectuals. This could mean leaving behind expected higher education practices (like the traditional university class structure) to create a new vision of a university class.
3. Bring together the teaching team, program head, and students to determine if a common framework is needed across classes/units in order to create spaces where students are safe to question, ponder, and act. If a framework is not needed, consider creating guiding principles for all teaching staff (permanent and part-time) to support safe spaces for dialogue and debate as well as taking risks and asking questions.
4. Bring together the teaching team, program head, and students to review the content in each class/unit to see if the content is a provocation to engage students as public intellectuals.

3. *Creating time to build a relationship with staff/faculty*

Relevant Policies and Structures: Timetabling, Tenure/Promotion, Staffing

While the student as consumer limits the possibilities of how the student-academic relationship can be implemented, the student as public intellectual provides limitless opportunities of how reciprocal relationships between students and academics can be imagined. With the change in traditional structures of classes, there are more opportunities for students to engage with the professor/lecturer. Support for consistent faculty (either permanent or adjunct/sessionals) across units/classes as well as built in time for meetings with students (small group, 1-on-1, etc.) can provide a frame for students to develop meaningful relationships with staff/faculty. Rethinking policies and traditions governing collaborations between students and staff/faculty offers unique perspectives on questions, ideas, and contestations within a field. For example, traditionally research and writing collaborations are between graduate students and staff/faculty. When undergraduate students begin their university experience in collaboration between staff/faculty, power dynamics are changed and students can be supported to further their comprehension of questions and current issues within a field.

Questions to consider:

1. In what ways are reciprocal relationships between students and academics supported and implemented in a program?
2. Are consistent part-time faculty used throughout a program? If not, does this impact building relationships between students and academics?
3. Are there opportunities for students and academics to come together with purpose? (For example, through a research project, community action, focus groups about curriculum)

Possible actions:

1. Rethink the student-academic relationship as a reciprocal relationship. Create ways to work reciprocally in classes/units and in experiences outside the usual student/teacher experience.
2. Consider how classes/units are staffed through permanent and part-time positions. Using the intent of building reciprocal relationships between student and academics, rethink staffing to support reciprocal relationships. If related policies and structures need revision to support this practice, engage in necessary revisions.
3. Offer formal opportunities for students to do research, write, or engage in community service/activities with academics. Again, related policies and structures may need revision to support in these practices.
4. Offer informal opportunities for students to engage with academics in discussion. For example, open coffee hours or similar.

4. *Participation of students in governance*

Relevant Policies and Structures: Student Code of Conduct, Use of Space/Facilities, Organizational Governance

In the current climate, student governance could be described as tokenistic. Students as consumers are given opportunities to engage with the decision-making but it is often on internal, very specific, and limiting resolution—athletic fees, student fees, control over certain facilities. It becomes more about administration checking a box next to student voice represented and does not carry on full and rich debate around issues regarding actual change. This action of checking the box, releasing the pressure of the administrator to include student opinion; this fake transparency manufactures consent to the administration. This type of students participation implies the view that students are incapable of thinking and offering genuine perspectives, expertise, or solutions. Not surprisingly, this reiterates the student as consumer.

When the student is viewed as public intellectual, a model of reciprocal relationships situated in trust and listening emerges between student and administrator. Students are involved from the beginning in discussions about issues regarding campus wide priorities and budget models. By creating a process designed (in collaboration between students and administration) and implemented across the university context that legitimately takes the knowledge and input by students and translates to action and policy, supports building the capacity of students and reverence of the student as more than just a means to money-making. One way to do this is to rethink and rewrite student codes of conduct with students aware first of how neoliberalism is reflected in each policy. Dialogues about which policies imply the student is consumer and which policies support the student as public intellectual grant develop students' awareness of how they are positioned and how these positions can be disrupted and rethought by rewriting policy. Consider how the management of physical space changes when students are public intellectuals—physical space becomes a powerful place where student collectives gather to think, challenge, and engage with the university and the public.

This kind of real engagement is messy and complex but it offers students the opportunity to take the stance, share wisdom, and perspective, and act as a contributing member to the university community. These practices as public intellectual empower students to engage beyond higher education and in the communities where they live and work as active, democratic citizens. The student as public intellectual practices hope and translates into people practicing hope in the local and global communities.

Questions to consider:

1. What kind of relationships exist between students and administration? What view of the student (consumer, public intellectual, something else?) underpins the relationships between students and administration?
2. What role do students play in decision-making at the university? Does this role in decision-making support students engaging as public intellectuals?
3. In what ways does the student code of conduct support students engaging as public intellectuals?
4. How are physical spaces managed for students? What is the intent of policies and procedures managing spaces? Can student gather in productive ways supportive of students as public intellectuals? What are the limitations of using spaces?

Possible actions:

1. Engage students in decisions regarding actual change at the university with the purpose of students engaging as public intellectuals. This includes offering students opportunities to participate in reviewing the current context, debate, and action.
2. Working collaboratively with students, rewrite the role of students in decision-making so there is a clear understanding of how students can contribute and act in the university context.
3. Review the current student code of conduct with students taking an active role in the review. Determine how the code of conduct supports students engaging as public intellectuals and revise (with students) any sections that do not support students engaging as public intellectuals.

4. Review any policies and procedures with students relating to space management. Determine the purpose of the policies and procedures supporting students engaging as public intellectuals. Revise (with students) any policies and procedures that do not support students engaging as public intellectuals.

References

Adler, S., & Iorio, J. M. (2015). Progressive teachers of young children: Creating contemporary agents of change. In M. Y. Eryaman & B. Bertram (Eds.), *International handbook of progressive education*. New York: Peter Lang Publishing Inc.

Adler, S., & Iorio, J. M. (2013). Progressive education: Past, present, and future: Progressive pedagogies in early childhood education. *International Journal of Progressive Education, 9*(2), 129–144.

Adler, S. M., & Iorio, J. M. (2012). Empowering teachers of young children: Moving students from agents of surveillance to agents of change. In J. Faulkner (Ed.), *Disrupting pedagogies and teaching the knowledge society: Countering conservative norms with creative approaches*. IGI Global: Hershey.

Blackmore, J. (1997). Disciplining feminism: A look at gender-equity struggles in Australian higher education. In L. Roman & L. Eyre (Eds.), *Dangerous Territories* (pp. 75–95). New York: Routledge.

Brulé, E. (2004). Neo-liberalism and the social construction of the university student as an autonomous consumer. In M. Reimer (Ed.), *Inside Corporate U: Women in the academy speak out* (pp. 247–264). Toronto: Sumach Press.

Brulé, E. (2015). Voices from the margins: The regulation of student activism in the New Corporate University. *Studies in Social Studies, 9*(2), 159–175.

Callaway-Cole, L., & Quintero, E.P. (2017). Unpublished manuscript. (Camarillo, CA).

Cote, M., de Peuter, G., & Day, R. (2007). *Utopian pedagogy: Radical experiments against neoliberal globalization*. Toronto: University of Toronto Press.

Cunningham (2016) Production of consumer spaces in the university. *Journal of Marketing for Higher Education, 26*(2), 199–213. https://doi.org/10.1080/08841241.2016.1238023

Davies, M., & Niemann, M. (2002). The everyday spaces of global politics: Work, leisure, family. *New Political Science, 24*(4), 557–577. https://doi.org/10.1080/0739314022000025390.

Edmundson, M. (1997). *On the uses of a liberal education: Part 1—As light entertainment for bored college students* (pp. 39–49). Sept: Harper's Magazine.

Giroux, H. (2006). Higher education under siege: Implications for public intellectuals. *Thought and Action,* 63–78.

Giroux, H. (2013). *America's education deficit and the war on youth: Reform beyond electoral politics*. New York: Monthly Review Press.

Griffith, A., & Smith, D. (2014). *Under new public management: Institutional ethnographies of changing frontline work*. Toronto: University of Toronto Press.

Greene, M. (1995). *Releasing the imagination: Essays on education, the arts, and social change*. San Francisco: Jossey-Bass.

Greene, M. (2001). The darkness and the light: Reconceiving the imagination. *Teachers and Writers, 33*(2), 29–30.

Hacker, A., & Dreifus, C. (2010). *Higher education? How colleges are wasting our money and failing our kids—And what we can do about it*. New York, NY: Times Books.

Hoeller, K. (Ed.). (2014). *Equality for contingent faculty: Overcoming the two-tiered system*. Nashville, TN: Vanderbilt University Press.

Ibbitson, J. (2000) York U strike all pain, no gain. *The Globe and Mail,* (14)B3

King, K. (2004). Historiography as reenactment: Metaphors and literalizations of TV documentaries. *Criticism, 46*(3), 459–475.

Latour, B. (2004). *The politics of nature: How to bring science into democracy*. Cambridge, MA: Harvard University Press.

Maringe, F. (2010). The student as consumer: Affordances and constraints in a transforming higher education environment. In M. Molesworth, R. Scullion, & E. Nixon (Eds.), *The marketisation of higher education and the student as consumer* (pp. 142–154). Oxon: Routledge.

Molesworth, M., Nixon, E., & Scullion, R. (2009). Having, being and higher education: The marketisation of the university and the transformation of the student into consumer. *Teaching in Higher Education, 14*(3), 277–287. https://doi.org/10.1080/13562510902898841.

Molesworth, M., Scullion, R., & Nixon, E. (Eds.). (2010). *The marketisation of higher education and the student as consumer*. London: Routledge.

Newson, J. A. (2004). Disrupting the 'student as consumer' model: The new emancipatory project. *International Relations, 18*(2), 227–229.

Pusey, A. (2016). Strike, occupy, transform! Students, subjectivity and struggle. *Journal of Marketing in Higher Education, 26*(2), 214–232. https://doi.org/10.1080/08841241.2016.1240133.

Quintero, E. (2009). *Critical literacy in early childhood education: Artful story and the integrated curriculum*. New York: Peter Lang.

Quintero, E. (2015). *Storying learning in early childhood: When children lead participatory curriculum design, implementation, and assessment*. New York: Peter Lang.

Quintero, E., & Rummel, M. (2003). *Becoming a teacher in the new society*. New York: Peter Lang.

Said, E. (1996). *Representations of the intellectual: The 1993 Reith lectures*. London, UK: Vintage Books.

Saunders, D. (2011). *Students as customers: The influence of neoliberal ideology and free-market logic on entering first-year college students*. Amherst, MA: University of Massachusetts.

Sealey-Huggins, L., & Pusey, A. (2013). Neoliberalism and depoliticisation in the academy: Understanding the 'new student rebellions'. *Graduate Journal of Social Science, 10*(3), 80–99.

Watts, V. (2013). Indigenous place-thought and agency amongst humans and non-humans (first woman and sky woman go on a European world tour!). *Decolonization: Indigeneity, Education & Society, 2*(1), 20–34.

Chapter 4
Academic as Public Intellectual

> *Some persons of a desponding spirit are in great concern about that vast number of academics using the university as a place to voice opinions, disrupt neoliberalism, and question the establishment under the guise of academic freedom, and we have been desired to employ our thoughts what course may be taken to ease higher education of so grievous an encumbrance. But we are not in the least pain upon that matter, because it is very well known that we can position these academics as service providers relieving them of academic freedom and putting them in their place by the neoliberal practices of efficiency, accountability, teaching evaluations, prescribed syllabi, university-wide templates, and class management systems. This way these academics have no time to think, and consequently pine away for want of intellectual nourishment to a degree that if at any time they are accidentally expected to ponder and engage, they have not the scholarly strength to perform it; and thus the university is happily delivered from the evils of the contemplative academic.*
>
> **The absurd:** *....But we are not in the least pain upon that matter, because it is very well known that we can position these academics as service providers relieving them of academic freedom and putting them in their place by the neoliberal practices of efficiency, accountability, teaching evaluations, prescribed syllabi, university-wide templates, and class management systems.*

Jeanne Marie keeps having this vision. It is the first day of classes for undergraduates at the university. As the academic teaching the class, she stands at the classroom door in a waitress uniform, complete with apron, hat, and roller skates. As each student enters the classroom, she hands them a menu. Available today are the following marks—A. B, C, D, F with the possibility of plus and minus as side orders. Once everyone takes a seat, she roller skates into the classroom holding a pen in one hand and a small pad in the other. She announces, "I will be by each of your seats, to take your orders for the semester." Slowly, she moves around the room, jotting down each student's order. Easily each student orders an A. Now, being the service provider she is, it is up to her to ensure their orders are completed and delivered to each student on a silver platter.

Sounds pretty absurd, right? Yet, when the student is constructed by the university context as consumer, the academic becomes the service provider (Newson, 2004)—essentially, the waitress serving grades to the customers. The satisfaction of the consumer dominates the relationship between student and academic. We believe this dynamic strongly impacts the curriculum and practice decisions made by faculty. Faculty under this framework may rethink the role that rigor plays in their teaching practice, and look for ways reinforce current student assumptions and beliefs, as opposed to testing them. This creates a new set of rules under which, for example, faculty begin to engage in a popularity contest where "best" is rewarded and defined by the customer. The best professors under this framework might be the "funniest" or the most "attractive" professors, or the easiest graders–but, perhaps not the professors that are the most "challenging" or those that expect the most. The academic in this sense becomes an expert in 'light entertainment' (Edmundson, 1997) rather than challenging students to think and engage in the process of coming "to understand themselves in the world through the curriculum they study" (Pinar, 2012, p. 44).

Back to Being a Waitress

Coming back to the waitress metaphor. Many food establishments have a comment card or nowadays, a website you can visit to complete a survey regarding the service received during your visit. Higher education has the same comment card/survey in the teaching evaluation distributed every semester for review of a course and as part of the review, evaluation of the academic/service provider/waitress by the student/consumer/customer. In particular, student evaluations of teaching (SET) are based on judging teacher effectiveness–yet, these very evaluations are not situated to complete this judgment (Boring, Ottoboni, & Stark, 2016; Stark, 2014) rather SET "measure what students say, and pretend it's the same thing" as teacher effectiveness (Stark, 2014, p. 9).

Boring et al. (2016) reviewed SET scores in an American university (43 SET for four sections of an online course) as well as a French University (23,001 SET of 379 instructors by 4423 students in six mandatory first-year courses) (p. 1) in a research project focused on SET regarding teaching teacher effectiveness. Findings include:

- identification of statistically significant bias in SET against female instructors (impacting ratings of objective aspects of teaching, varied by disciple and gender of student, non-adjustable because of large amount of factors establishing the bias),
- SET reflective more of grade expectations and gender bias of students rather than effectiveness, and
- Substantial amounts of gender bias in SET—"large enough to cause more effective instructors to get lower SET than less effective instructors."
(p. 2)

Other research and literature further supports the bias against female instructors in the SET (AAUP, 2015; Flaherty, 2016; MacNell, Driscoll, & Hunt, 2015; Schmidt, 2015; Schuman, 2014) and often includes racial bias and stereotypes. Phillips (2016), an Aboriginal woman and lecturer at Queensland Institute of Technology, shares how the comments in her SET reflect negative stereotypes of Indigenous peoples and seem to further perpetuate how SET does not consider how race and gender influence views of students on teachers.

Jakobi (2016) an Aboriginal teacher educator at Victoria University in Melbourne, Australia notes how his work is

> in interrogating, and unsettling structural privilege and racism that has subjected, and situated Australian First Peoples to sometimes fourth world conditions, needs to directly implicate the teacher educator learner, in order to better prepare them as teachers in their engagement with Aboriginal learners and their communities. This task requires provocation, not performance.

Yet, he recognises that in the context of neoliberalism, the intention of "Aboriginal sovereignty and self determination" have been ousted to entertain and perform, miming "the borders of our capacity to authentically engage learners beyond the redistributive frames regulated by the oppressor." These examples hark back to the concept of the customer–genderless, raceless, classless—with only the purpose of satisfaction in mind. Is it as simple as this–as long as students are satisfied with the service providers, sexism, racism, colonialism, and classism are okay?

Further Commitments to Neoliberalism

Other structures and commitments in higher education continue to further cement neoliberalism as how higher education is constructed. The rise of teaching-only and non-tenured appointments and an over-reliance on part-time lecturers in adjuncts and sessionals continues to dominate teaching (Aronowitz, 2000; Saunders, 2011; Slaughter & Rhoades, 2004). The perpetuation of the purpose of degrees as workforce development (Holzer, 2015; Lester & Costley, 2010). Academics working to bring in in money through grants and corporate contracts, framing knowledge by the intentions of the funder (Fraser & Taylor, 2016), further repositioning the academic as technician and grant writer.

The fear and manipulation of faculty through a false-sense of voice runs rampant—and then results in punishing faculty when they disagree with administration suggested mandates. For example, as administration increasingly works in the return-on-investment mode, academics are expected to teach more, lessen the cost of part-time workers, revising workload models to reflect more teaching, less research, and more service. Administration creates a culture of fear, suggesting that if the workload model is not approved and implemented, the doors of the university will close. "Contesting the very processes that so many senior university executives are promoting can be interpreted as acts of interpersonal disloyalty" (Fraser & Taylor, 2016, p. 17). This fear and manipulation is neoliberalism—as only one option is available according to administration. And this is the only way to ensure you still have a job, the university stays open, and higher education meets its mandate to educate many more students than it currently does.

A devotion to efficiency (Bromell, 2002) and adherence to structures becomes the practice of the academic where student satisfaction rules and limits academic response and action. This creates a context of restrictions where academic freedom is a novelty. For example, instead of the faculty being in charge of writing and revising syllabi on their own accord reflective of their expertise and current issues in the field, universities are often governed by a large web-based central system managing all approvals and day-to-day management of courses and the subsequent units or courses. This system standardizes every course and unit and demonstrates compliances as related to policy both at the local (university) and national level. Most universities have these systems in place with the purpose of protecting 'the university from potential litigation' (Newson, 2004, p. 231) from the students acting as consumers. Faculty are required to complete the standardized system for every unit/course so any sort of flexibility or ability to respond to students the academic might employ is sacrificed in the name of consumer demand.

As a service provider in the big business of higher education, the academic is forced to accept the student as consumer as well as perpetuate the role of service provider to these customers. Any unsettling or disruption to a student's values or beliefs (even if founded in falsehoods and stereotypes) is viewed as dissatisfaction because of the structures and tools within the university are simplistic and only recognise satisfaction as constructed by the typical consumer. This builds a specific type of relationship between student/customer and academic/service provider and illustrates the acceptance (and in some cases, unwilling acceptance) of the neo-liberal agenda and the assumption of academics being powerless within the university context. In what ways might academics resist and find voice in a context that constantly implements and continues to support neoliberal policy and procedure?

Disrupting the Absurd: The Academic as Public Intellectual

Through the practice of hope, we rethink the academic as public intellectual. This rethinking disrupts and rethinks the academic as service provider, offering a way to resist and give voice to the academic, "Thus, communities are not seen as composed of passive receptacles into which 'expert' knowledge might be poured, but of active living human subjects, possessed of ways of seeing, speaking, thinking, acting, and imagining" (Cote Day, & de Peuter, 2007, p. 322). Using Said's (1996) concept of the public intellectual, academics as public intellectuals raise questions that may not be welcomed, face accepted practices and dominant doctrines head on, and resist the influence of corporation so present in universities and are "actively willing" to engage publicly (Said, 1996, p. 23) and recognise that exile, misalignment, and marginality are also a possibility. While exile, misalignment, and marginality may seem as limiting, it may also be a privilege as it creates space where the ethics and politics of teaching, learning, and acting in the world can be developed and complexified, connecting across disciplines and with the local and global communities. Further, ideas and assumptions can be challenged and rethought, often engaging without the interference of what neoliberalism brings the university context.

We understand that the university already is a neoliberal context and established discourses and hierarchies continue to influence teaching, learning, leadership and decision-making (Giroux, 2013). Highly aware of this context, we still believe the rethinking of the academic as public intellectual is a possibility to reclaiming higher education as an ethical and political place where neoliberalism is questioned, critical thinking is the norm, and democracy is at the forefront of teaching and learning.

Academics as public intellectuals are committed—committed to their beliefs, values, and thinking beyond the expected, "commitment should rule education; not consumerism" (Greene, 2012). This sense of commitment constructs teaching as "rigorous, self-reflective, and committed not to the dead zone of instrumental rationality but to the practice of freedom, to a critical sensibility capable of advancing the parameters of knowledge, addressing crucial social issues, and connecting private troubles and public issues" (Giroux, 2013, p. 46)—engaging the academic as "critical educator and active citizen" (p. 46). Greene (1978) referred to this as "wide awakeness"—"awareness of what it is to be in the world" (Greene, 1995, p. 35). When the academic as public intellectual is wide-awake in Greene's (1995, 2000, 2005) sense, she creates a space for herself and her students to be cognizant of how power and knowledge construct the world and how this impacts equity across local and global communities. Further, academics as public intellectuals are empathetic beyond themselves and deeply aware of current neoliberal context–mindful of how as educators they "must be awake, critical, open to the world. It is an honor and a responsibility to be a teacher in such dark times—and to imagine, and to act on what we imagine, what we believe ought to at last be" (Greene, 2005, p. 80).

Wide-Awake, Committed, and a Collective

I sit with three academics, two established scholars (full professors) and an emerging scholar (lecturer/assistant professor). We sit in a restaurant, away from the large international research conference taking place and the reason for why we can be together in this restaurant. This is an international group, representative of both the United States and Australia. Drink and food orders are placed and then all eyes are on me as I have asked each of them to join me in a dialogue about how each of them engage as a public intellectual. Clif and I have known each of these of people for a while and we have seen how they engage with the public—how they ask questions and constantly interrupt the dogmas dictating how a teacher educator is expected to be in the higher education classroom. We want to know if they think of themselves as public intellectuals and how they might define this in their work and their context.

"Two-pronged" is how a full professor at an American public university immediately shares—for her the public intellectual is not just about the academic but

also viewing the undergraduate student as public intellectual. Knowledge, wisdom, responsibility are all used to describe this view of both the academic and student. She notes that not every academic she works with in the school of education shares her view, then bluntly stating, "I don't give a fuck of what colleagues think of me" further describing how her work has always been driven by activism and advocacy. Her roots in the field go back to work with Paulo Freire and have continued in collaboration with local communities, migrants, and refugees. For this public intellectual, the local and global communities are connected and she can be found working with refugees in European cities and cities local to her university in the United States. "Collectivism" is how she describes this work—and it moves into her early childhood teacher education course. Her undergraduate students engage in assignments that document the lives and stories of migrant and refugee families. These lives and stories are central to how teaching is imagined for these emerging teachers. The expectations this academic demands of herself are the same she demands of her students—to listen and respond to community where they are, as a collective. There is power in the collective.

The collective is something that becomes a point of agreement across the group as food arrives, tastes are shared, and the conversation continues. The other professor at the table, also representative of an American public university describes the collective as a think tank—a think tank he brings together himself and his graduate assistants as group of public intellectuals. This is what he identifies as an "entry point" into articulating the public intellectual space. The creation of this space offers access, an affordance of a space to engage as a public intellectual. He finds it is a "negotiated space" that changes dependent on the issues, conversations, and questions emerging. There is a recognition of how acting as a public intellectual can be "counter" to what neoliberalism dictates as the job of the academic. And maybe even sometimes acting as a public intellectual could support a reclusive-sense of self, outside of the limitations of being the neoliberal intellectual.

"Imposter!" this word is thrown out into the table......and then explained. You know, you may think you are a public intellectual, but are you really? Are you just an imposter trying to question, trying to challenge, trying to engage the public with the relevant issues? And then someone points out how the stories we share give meaning to the public intellectual—stories steeped in empathy for people and communities beyond the university walls. Stories full of passion and aware of the gaps in the world. Stories about action and collectivism.

The lecturer/assistant professor speaks up and shares her story—a story about how even after teaching within early childhood teacher education programs for years, she began to rethink, making a space for contention, questioning, and challenge for herself and her students. She talks about not conforming—but knowing the rules well enough to rethink and even break them. She articulates reciprocal teaching and the use of learning circles. Again, the collective comes up evident in the shared power of reciprocal teaching and learning circles where students and the academic are public intellectuals.

Wide-Awake and Writing

Teachers College Record is a "journal of research, analysis, and commentary in the field of education. It has been published continuously since 1900 by Teachers College, Columbia University" (https://www.tcrecord.org/About.asp). Commentaries are a welcome submission to the journal as a way to inspire dialogue in education about current issues. An invitation on the *Teachers College Record* commentary web page issues a provocation,

> You are invited to add your unique voice and perspective to a vibrant, forward thinking conversation around some of the most timely topics in the education sector. We welcome sophisticated commentary, similar to that found in the world's leading publications, that covers a wide range of education related topics and draws fresh connections to contemporary issues. As a contributor you will both be invited to discuss topics of our choosing and have the exciting opportunity to create content of your choice around subjects that interest you as both a scholar and practitioner. Let's work together to move the conversation around education further into the future while reframing and evaluating scholarship of the past.
>
> (https://www.tcrecord.org/Opinion.asp)

There are several ways to contribute to sharing your voice through the commentary including suggesting a topic, volunteering to write a commentary, and submitting a commentary. Through 1500 words, commentary authors engage and provoke, discussing and debating policy, decisions, practices, and other topics that offer readers a way towards "wide-awakeness" (Greene, 1978). Strong commentaries have a well-constructed argument, offer a diversity of opinions, and provoke debate and dialogue, according to Brian Sweeting, Digital Publishing Editor, *Teachers College Record* (Personal Conversation, 2017). Commentaries are featured in the *Teachers College Record* newsletter, a source freely available to anyone that signs up to receive the newsletter. Free access to the commentaries is offered through the newsletter and commentaries reflect current topical issues encouraging many reads of specific commentaries.

Relevant Issues in the Field Discussed

Specific current topics are often the subject across several commentaries. For example, the implementation of the Teacher Performance Assessment (edTPA) evoked much writing. Teacher educators Jordan and Hawley (2016) share how the edTPA and those that support the implementation perform injustices against vulnerable teacher candidates. "The Dangerous Message Teacher Candidates Infer: "If the edTPA Does Not Assess It, I Don't Have to Do It" (Soslau et al., 2015) brings together an assistant professor and two field instructors discussing what is measured and valued through the edTPA. In particular, they note how the edTPA is interpreted as checklist of skills and how often teacher candidates limit their understanding of practice only through this list with little or no indications of understanding that teaching includes competencies beyond list. Conley and Garner (2015) use implementation scenarios of the edTPA and teacher preparation to discuss the de-skilling of teachers as well as the possibilities the edTPA could offer.

A continued dialogue initiated by one commentary, offers multiple perspectives on the edTPA. The commentary "Who's Preparing our Candidates? edTPA, Localized Knowledge and the Outsourcing of Teacher Evaluation" (Dover, Schultz, Smith, & Duggan, 2015b) critiques the edTPA and received a huge response from teachers educators, faculty, and administrators from the across the country. Comments on the commentary appearing on the *Teachers College Record* website next to the commentary include:

> Brilliant piece, based on sound teacher learning research with a touch of 70 s-Geraldo-undercover journalism.
>
> (Margolis, April 3, 2015)
>
> The schema of teacher credentialing would need to undergo a transformation if education preparation programs solely kept control of the process. That is, the EPP would need to track candidates into the profession & collaborate with school personnel to determine who is qualified for licensure recommendation. It would seem that three years would be needed to vet this process. I am not suggesting a capitulation to recent CAEP inanity, but it would take a Herculean effort to keep the process in-house in order to ensure that our candidates meet a 360° assessment of competency. If we cannot manage such a feat, then we invite EdTPA's and other Pearson content and pedagogy tests to replace what we (EPP) are not able to do. I do think that regional scoring of EdTPA portfolios might off-set the cottage industries and provide more local control of the process. Regional scoring by faculty would also enable greater insight into program improvement and collaboration across EPP's.
>
> Perhaps it is time for higher education to learn from K-12 parents and students and learn how to OPT OUT (or better yet–REFUSE) all of this bs....
>
> (Somers, April 4, 2015)

While some of the respondents shared in the same perspective of the authors, a formal rebuttal commentary was also a part of the responses (Adkins, Spesia, & Snakenborg, 2015),

> written by faculty and administrators who have been instrumental in the development and promulgation of edTPA policy at the local and national level, and now act as spokespeople for edTPA (e.g., Adkins, Haynes, Pringle, Renner, & Robinson, 2013; Layzell & Adkins, 2012; Spesia, 2015; Snakenborg, 2014). Their rebuttal challenges our evidence and logic, using their experience as edTPA scorers, consultants, and policymakers to support the validity of edTPA as a national, high stakes assessment (Dover et al., 2015b).

Dover et al. (2015a) then continues the conversation with another commentary following the rebuttal, focusing on the relationships edTPA between profit, scholarship, and policy. The authors note, "regardless of developers" initial intent, it seems the speed of edTPA implementation—fueled largely, perhaps, by the intense profitability of the privatization of teacher preparation—has both outpaced and precluded scholarly engagement." The commentary ends with a call for "continued scholarship" in order to build a "sound, peer-reviewed research base" that informs the implementation and understands both the "professional and fiscal consequences for candidates."

Commentaries as Provocation

Commentaries are a means of provocation for academics. For example, the commentary "Engaging with Ethical Resistance and Courageous Activism: A Response to Where Do I Fit In? Adrift in Neoliberal Educational Anti-Culture" (Hamm et al., 2017) is in response to a previous commentary "Where Do I Fit In? Adrift in Neoliberal Educational Anti-Culture" (Burns, 2016). Burns's commentary recognises higher education as a "neoliberal educational anti-culture" and asks the questions of "where do I fit" and "where do I find hope" in this current state. As a collective, the early childhood faculty at Victoria University in Melbourne, Australia considered these questions and pondered how they are coming to work in this "anti-culture" providing examples of resistance and action defined as Burns's "ethical resistance" and "courageous activism". This exchange between commentaries illustrates how commentaries can provide a space for debate and dialogue among readers, creating a forum for anyone to question, consider, and rethink issues and ideas. Digital Publishing Editor Brian Sweeting adds, "Not everyone needs to be an education researcher" to write a commentary (Personal Conversation, 2017) and authors include practicing teachers creating a platform for connecting the university to the public. For example, an upcoming topic specifically asks for K-12 teacher perspective, "Teachers' commentaries provide an important perspective on current educational issues. If you are a K-12 educator, we welcome you to submit a 1000–1500 word commentary in which you draw on your experience to address problems and opportunities confronting students and educators" (https://www.tcrecord.org/Opinion.asp).

Commentary Writing Building a Collective

Recently, commentary writing for *Teachers College Record* has been the impetus to bring together academics from around the world to write as a collective. An initiative through the Critical Perspectives on Early Childhood Education (CPECE) Special Interest Group (SIG), American Educational Research Association (AERA), invites academics to submit and write about relevant topics to the field. "We would like to initiate both discussions and publications through this part of the website to encourage emerging academics and scholars in the field to collaborate together as well as offer perspectives beyond our SIG audience to the public" (https://sites.google.com/site/cpecesig/blog). The process includes submitting topics, volunteering to write, sharing the commentary with the SIG for further comments and writing, and then submitting to *Teachers College Record* for possible publication. Since 2017, commentaries published consider quality in early childhood education and its relationship to the Teacher Performance Assessment (edTPA) (Peters, Reinke, & Castner, 2017), teachers for social justice (Garlen, Kuh, & Coleman 2017), and the lack of participation and representations of people of color in professional critical organisations (Axelrod et al., 2018).

Wide-Awake and Researching

Fraser and Taylor (2016) outline the production of knowledge in the neoliberal context of the university,

> Academics are no longer esteemed for being public intellectuals committed to general public discourse on crucial issues and/or collaborating with community partners. Instead, we are constituted as commercial agents expected to pursue commercially viable projects, sometimes with the help of specially designated intermediaries (Kauppinen, 2012). We are increasingly expected to fund-raise research resources and solicit mediate attention to enhance our 'profile." If this happens to incorporate social justice or social change goals—all the better—because that too can be marketable and profit raising, helping to create a veneer of respectability; one that covers commercial interests to portray more palatable images of universities as noble places of knowledge and learning.
>
> (pp. 10–11)

As the commodification of knowledge continues to grow across higher education, research agendas addressing social and global issues are often placed in the margin. Academics are deemed successful when awarded large grants and publishing in high-ranked journals. This neoliberal framework removes the public and any connection beyond the walls of higher education. Further, what is considered legitimate knowledge is what can be measured, giving power to numeric evidence situated in a positivist paradigm (Fraser & Taylor, 2016).

Academics acting as public intellectuals calls for an alternative means of creating and implementing research agendas. Moss (2016) suggests "meaning-making" as a way to rethink quality in early childhood research. Meaning-making moves from the expected positivist stance of "regulatory modernity" and provides a lens to make meaning "in relationship with others, in processes of co-construction, processes that involve dialogue, reflection, contestation and interpretation." We take inspiration from Moss's "meaning-making" and situate meaning-makes as being wide-awake in the world and engaging as Said (1996) describes "public intellectuals" aware of our values and acting in an ethical manner with the purpose of moving towards humanity and equity. For example, Dryden-Peterson (2016) connects the current situation of refugee education to her research agenda. She examines refugee education from World War II to the present attempting "how to realise the right to education for all and ensure opportunities to use that education for future participation in society" (p. 473). In terms of democracy, Levy, Solomon, and Collet-Gildard (2016) study the political interest of United States high-school students in relationship to the 2012 United States Presidential Election. This work contributes directly to the construction of a democratic society as understanding how high-school students engage in political activities impacts how the voter is constructed and could possibly contribute. These examples illustrate academics as public intellectuals, making meaning through research agendas.

Storying: Impact and Engagement with Issues of Social Justice

Elizabeth Quintero has always chosen to situate her research in social justice. Her qualitative research follows educators, families, community elders, and teachers and through the use of storying, offering concrete illustrations of advocacy and activism. As part of the Bilingual Family Literacy Project in Texas, family literacy project in Minnesota with Hmong and Somali families, and her experiences with refugee families seeking asylum in Ankara, Turkey, she gathers her research to tell powerful stories. For us, these stories illustrate how she is wide-awake to issues of social justice and this awakeness drives her desire to document these voices. Other ongoing projects including working with families of Asylum Seekers, collaborations with Refugee Council, and continued work with families in New York City representative of Latino, Syrian, Palestinian, Pakistani, Orthodox Russian Jewish, and Central American families. Recently, she spent time with Nigerian refugee women in Verona, Italy. She shares her work as a teacher educator engaging with her pre-service teachers as critical to students understanding place and how place impacts the lives of migrant and refugee families. Her research is found in the higher education classroom as well as in her developed texts on critical literacy and storying, representing how multiple languages, knowledges, and identities contribute to meaning-making within the field and community (Quintero 2009, 2011, 2017; Quintero & Rummel, 2014).

Out and About: Local and Global Issues of Sustainability

Across a local primary school, weekly and every fortnight, children between the ages of 5 and 11, walk with their teachers to different outdoor places within the community with the intention of thinking *with* the place as a means of building a relationship between humans and the earth (Blaise, Hamm, & Iorio, 2016; Iorio, Coustley, & Grayland, 2018; Iorio, Hamm, Parnell, & Quintero, 2017). The research project "Out and About" focuses on the teaching pedagogies educators enact as part of building relationship with place. With two sites, one in a regional coastal town in Victoria, Australia and another in urban Melbourne, this research considers the devastating current human-induced state of the environment (Solomon, Plattner, Knutti, & Friedlingstein, 2009) and how this illustrates a lack of relationship between humans and the earth. Out and About links directly with community and public concerns regarding sustainability and supports the building relationships between humans and planet in order to reshape the futures of the local and global environments. Framed by 'common world' pedagogies (www.commonworlds.net; Taylor & Guigini, 2012; Taylor & Pacini-Ketchabaw, 2015), this research seeks to understand how teachers support children in learning from relationships in their 'common' worlds with the human and the more-than-human in order to rethink common futures.

Place is integral factor in the Out and About research project. For this research, place is understood as a "territory that is Indigenous and which has been and continues to be subject to the forces of colonization" (Tuck, McKenzie, & McCoy, 2014, p. 1). Place from this perspective reminds the researchers and educators to be attentive to entanglements of place, noting how historical, ethical, and political facets are always present and informing the place.

Walking, listening, smelling, talking, touching inform the multisensory "place-making" methods (Pink, 2008) used in this project. The contact zone (Haraway, 2008) in this research is place and focuses the work noticing the relations between the more-than-human and human (Hamm & Boucher, 2018). Practices like pedagogical documentation (Dahlberg, Moss, & Pence, 2007; Edwards, Gandini, & Forman, 1998; Parnell, 2011; Rinaldi, 2006) completed by teachers and researchers as well field notes, and reflections across the research process contribute to data collection. Pedagogical documentation works to make place and the relationships with more-than-human visible. For example, over 100 six- and seven-year-old children visit Fishermans Beach, located about a 30 min walk from school. The educators walk, listen, smell, wonder, converse with the children throughout these moments and then create documentation panels sharing the essence of these experiences, making visible the place as well as the children's and educator's thinking and listening *with* the place. These panels are shared across the school and in public spaces as a provocation for debate and dialogue in the school and local community. Latour's (2005) notions of tracing and assembling, and paying attention to the unexpected guide on-going analysis of the data.

Wide-Awake and Committed to the Public Good

In Australia: The Brisbane Declaration

The University of Queensland and Friends of the Earth with support from the National Tertiary Education Union (NTEU), National Alliance for Public Universities (NAPU), and the Ngara Institute organised a conference Challenging the Privatised University in November 2015 to discuss the current context of the university system. Of particular focus was the infiltration of corporations into higher education, impacting both research and teaching (Hill, 2016). Academics gathered at the conference were wide-awake to the large amount of literature concluding the present neoliberal conditions in the university but now wanted to have "a public conversation about alternatives to this system and what might constitute a 'good university'" (p. 5).

Creating an "academic activist culture" became the recommendation of the conference participants. This culture would support actions including,

> Finding ways of re-engaging with colleagues across disciplines, building collegial, democratic cultures within schools and departments, discussing corporate influence and what to do about it, encouraging colleagues to join the National Tertiary Education Union (NTEU) and the National Alliance for Public Universities (NAPU), and undertaking research for the public rather than private gain.
>
> (Hill, 2016, p. 6)

Further, the conference participants developed a public statement "The Brisbane Declaration" expressing the infrastructure of a 'good university'—"The declaration is intended as a watershed statement to guide future campaigns in the struggle to create a genuine and fully funded public university system" (p. 6). The declaration reads:

THE BRISBANE DECLARATION

Given the role of multinational corporations in contributing to the looming global environmental, social and financial crises; and their increasing influence on all forms of education, including university education, there has never been a more important time to rethink the meaning of a good university in Australia.

Good universities are:

- Communities not for-profit corporations;
- Democratic public institutions for the social good;
- Fully funded by government;
- Independent of corporate influence;
- Dedicated to offering free, high quality education;
- Transparent and accountable;
- Transformational not merely transactional;
- Democratically accountable to society as a whole;
- Committed to an ethical and knowledge driven curriculum that fosters critical reflection and creativity.

Good universities:

- Embrace multiple ways of knowing;
- Nurture public intellectuals;
- Promote the free exchange of ideas in the quest for truth;
- Actively value collegiality and collaboration;
- Uphold and support the role of student unions;
- Uphold diversity in the production of knowledge;
- Foster and develop mutual respect;
- Participate in the development of a just, democratic and sustainable society which privileges ecologies over the economy;
- Empower students to become active citizens and not just job ready graduates;
- Explicitly incorporate an understanding of indigenous culture and history;
- Recognise and integrate bodies of knowledge from the global south;
- Recognise academic freedom as a core value;
- Produce open, available and accessible knowledge;
- Include all academic and non-academic staff, and students as active participants in decision-making processes and culture;
- Invite alternative, non-hierarchical and respectful forms of performance review.

> This declaration is intended to spark a national conversation about the nature, role and purpose of university education in a socially just, democratic society. We invite reflection, debate and dialogue in pursuit of the good university.
>
> (2016, p. 5)

The Brisbane Declaration is an example of academics wide-awake to the issues impacting the context of higher education and beyond. With a commitment to nurturing public intellectuals, empowering students, and understanding how higher education impacts society and democracy, this document reflects the power of a collective while participants in this conference act as public intellectuals.

In the United States: CReATE

A network of academics representative of Chicago-area universities came together through the leadership of Dr. Kevin Kumashiro to further public understanding of education as the Chicagoland Researchers and Advocates for Transformative Education (CReATE) (http://www.createchicago.org/). Experts in educational research, these academics partner with community-based organizations, teachers, and other public interest groups to create spaces for dialogue, debate, and learning about education. Real issues to Chicago schools are discussed including school closure, teachers evaluations, high-stakes testing, and school reforms. Writing factsheets, research briefs, and letters, the collective comes together to empower the public to make informed decisions regarding policy and advocacy.

An example of CReAte's work is the policy statement *Chicago School Reform: Myths, Realities, and New Visions* (2015). This statement sharing how reforms in Chicago during the Mayor Emanuel's term have impacted the community, families, and children served. The statement,

> outlines a democratic, equitable, and research-backed vision that provides the Chicago school community a set of policy alternatives to the myths that too often are simply claimed without supporting evidence to be real solutions to Chicago's education challenges. The research we share supports and affirms many of the key criticisms, popular goals, and workable alternatives to the current CPS policies that are continuing to be challenged by local parent, community, and teacher organizations.
>
> (p. 1)

Discussion of the repercussions of the policies implemented and alternatives are presented as part of the statement. The discussion includes several sections beginning with the Vision CReAte offers, then detailing the Myth and Reality related to the vision. Research Supported Action Goals follow articulating actions that reach the proposed Vision. Finally, the section lists a group of educational researchers available for comment for this specific vision. Below is an example of one section from the policy statement,

> **Vision**: Develop and Implement Education Policy and Reform Initiatives that are Primarily Community-, Learner- and Research-driven, Not Consumer- and Market-driven.

Myth: Because competition leads to improvement, school "choice" options are necessary, and because the private sector can do better than public schools, consumer-based "choice" options must involve privatization of education.

Reality: Philanthropies, dominated by a handful of foundations that advance initiatives of choice, competition, deregulation, accountability tied to standardized test scores, and the dismantling of teacher unions, altogether spend almost $4 billion annually, with an increasing proportion going toward policy advocacy at the national level. In some cases, poorer neighborhoods in Chicago saw reductions in funding even while enrollments rose, and there is evidence that choice exacerbates racial segregation and reduces opportunities for greater educational equity. School-choice, voucher, and restrictive-enrollment programs have not proven to be more effective in increasing district overall student achievement. Furthermore, there is clear evidence that choice programs exacerbate racial segregation. Overall, the private sector has not proven more effective at improving schools, despite a rapid increase in expenditures for outsourcing services and products including school management, curriculum, and assessments. The majority of charter schools are seriously underfunded, spending $400–$1400 less per pupil on instruction than neighborhood schools.

Research Supported Action Goals:

- Draw on the expertise of educators and researchers, not primarily the business and philanthropy sectors, to develop policies and reforms.
- Suspend the school-turnaround and closure process, then develop and apply standards for school restructuring that are research-based, consistent, fair, and transparent.
- Enforce policies for public accountability, and require all schools that are supported by public funds to constitute Local School Councils with a voting majority of parents.
- Provide district leaders who are knowledgeable about education and urban contexts and skillful in collaborative and democratic decision-making processes, continue in the future with a credentialed
- superintendent for CPS, and transition from mayoral control to a democratically elected school board that is accountable to the public

(pp. 3–4)

The policy statement ends with a section indicating a "way forward". In three paragraphs, CReAte states exactly how the school system, school, teachers, and students should be supported and created. "Education would act in the real world, and thus the value of the learning and action would be palpable for each student. Students would be honored for their ability to think new things, to see advantages and disadvantages, to work together, to build a better society" (p. 8). This section makes visible to the public the possibility and potential of school, presenting a concrete "way forward" based on the detailed discussion of the facts of the situation and real actions and solutions. In this policy statement, it is evident of what is possible when academics commit to equity and ensuring the public is aware so action can be a reality.

In United States: Leaders for the Next Generation

In the University of Hawai'i system (3 universities, 7 community colleges and community-based learning centers across Hawai'i) a similar program exists, Leaders for the Next Generation (LNG). Funded by a private endowment, LNG participants represent the entire system and include faculty, staff, and recent College of Education graduates with interest in community engagement and educational leadership. LNG offers opportunities for members to intern and build professional relationships with community leaders from business, legislative, educational, and non-profit settings, identify and strengthen natural leadership skills and interests, and establish a network of supportive emerging leadership partners.

Under Clif's leadership, LNG developed and implemented an annual group-wide "Community Give Back Project." The idea behind the Give Back Project is to leverage the considerable talents and energies of the LNG participants to make meaningful and tangible contributions to the community and to education in Hawai'i. Critical to this work was creating a space for faculty to see and understand themselves as public/community leaders—connecting their work beyond the university context as understanding and committing to action that service and contributes to the local community. Through two phases, the Give Back Project includes research, dialogue, and a process for creating a plan of action regarding a specific issue to address (phase 1) and then implement the action plan (phase 2).

One example of a Give Back Project focused on the issue of parental engagement in public education in response to a local furlough action and related protest against the furlough. LNG created the Forum on Engagement in Public Education, in partnership with two local community-based education organizations, The Learning Coalition and Hawai'i Education Matters, to lead an island-wide conversation on the state of parental engagement in Hawai'i's public schools. The Forum included a panel of community stakeholders, principals representing the public schools and faculty. For purposes of context, a research presentation was delivered regarding parent involvement in public education. Attendance at the forum included state legislators, board of education members, union leaders, business leaders, gubernatorial candidates, executive directors of community family and education organizations, representatives from the Hawai'i Department of Education and the University of Hawai'i. This event provoked the public to action including establishing a leadership team and building a more very influential coalition named HE'E (Hui for Excellence in Education) focusing on improving support and engagement in public education in Hawai'i.

Story 1: A Collective of Public Intellectuals Disrupting and Rethinking Policies and Structure at Victoria University, Australia

Making visible the collective of public intellectuals is a powerful tool in disrupting the neoliberal context of higher education. While structures in the university support the individual academic for success in the neoliberal university, we contend that the collective is how neoliberalism can be unsettled and revised. In our research project at Victoria University, Melbourne, *Rethinking Structures and Policies with the VU Early Childhood Course,* the group of early childhood teacher educators choose to make visible their work as a collective. We come together to create a space of ethical resistance–a place where we discuss and respond to issues in the field, think and analyze policy, procedure, and research, attend university-wide meetings, and question accepted practices and checklists narrowing the university to a profit-driven institution. Examples of this work include published commentaries responding to government reports and sanctions (Agius et al., 2015a; Hamm et al., 2017) and an invited article in a professional magazine influential across early childhood in Australia (Agius et al., 2015b).

Collective Publications

These publications offer ways in which we are rethinking the structures and policies in higher education at Victoria University. In "Who's Swallowing the *Action Now: Classroom Ready Teachers* Report? Discussing, Understanding, and Wondering" (Agius et al., 2015a), we discuss *Action Now: Classroom Ready Teachers* (2015) report released by the Teacher Education Ministerial Advisory Group (TEMAG), a report focused on establishing specific regulations in teacher education. Yet, the report does not include any discussion of early childhood. The absence of early childhood becomes the fodder for discussion for these early childhood teacher educators and leads to a commentary focusing on wonderings, evidence, language, and implied meanings. For us,

> We are concerned that this report has been consumed as "truth" without being fully digested or understood by the public. At the same time, we consider how this report opens up spaces for dialogue about early childhood education, often not at the table and as an after-thought in policymaking and education agendas. Our collective resistance to accepting the generalized findings and recommendations as presented in the report positions us to disrupt blind acceptance of dogmas within education and to re-think teacher education as a place where teachers think, question, and practice as agents of change—the critical practice we hope our early childhood teacher education students will implement in their classrooms, and unfortunately, is absent in this report and any of the subsequent actions.

Action comes out of this collective publication as the group of early childhood teacher educators are invited by Australian College of Educators' (ACE) publication *Professional Educator* to write about what "classroom ready" might be for early childhood educators, in response to the absence of early childhood in the report *Action Now: Classroom Ready Teacher* and our related commentary in *Teacher College Record*. This journal "aims to bring together the educational research and practice of all educators across all systems as well as policy and its effects 'on the ground' in a way that is readable, that speaks to all in the education field and that stimulates debate" (http://www.austcolled.com.au/products/professional-educator). The impetus of this work is to suggest teachers "being present" are classroom ready teachers. Being present is about being wide-awake and open to engaging as an agent of change, willing recognizing that "all teaching is political and must identify practices of oppression, moments of empowerment, and everything in-between" (p. 11). These ideas directly impact the university structure of course outcomes.

The collective's third publication came out of a government report *Working together to shape teacher education in Victoria* (2016) from the Victorian State Minister of Education and inspiration from a commentary in *Teachers College Record*, "Where do I fit in? Adrift in neoliberal anti-culture" (Burns, 2016). The government paper was written in response to suggested recommendations regarding Australian initial teacher education in *Action Now: Classroom Ready Teachers Report* (Teacher Education Ministerial Advisory Group, 2014). As a college of education, we were asked to respond to the government report *Working together to shape teacher education in Victoria* (2016). The action of responding to this report in terms of our own context as well as other ways we were acting as a collective seemed to be articulated through Burn's (2016) commentary through his descriptions of "hope" and "ethical resistance". We found a connection to his words, "Working toward an unknowable future in ethically and intellectually bankrupt institutions that privilege narrowly defined intelligence through the hubris of data and technological rationalization is difficult and dangerous work" and the recommendations demanded on teacher education by the government report. And so our third collective publication began as a response to Burns's commentary—we wanted to talk about how we fit in, how we were resisting, and how we were hoping to reverse the fatalistic context of the neoliberal university,

> At times this work is challenging as we continually come up against neo-liberal structures and policies in our work as academics. As a growing collective, we will continue our work to create spaces for ethical resistance, not just by disrupting structures, but by also offering ways to re-think. We are committed to finding ethical ways to work in higher education that privilege Aboriginal knowledges, position students and academics as public intellectuals and generate new spaces to resist obsession with the technical aspects of teaching and learning.
>
> (Hamm et al., 2017)

Collective Rethinking Course Outcomes

Course outcomes are created for every program at Victoria University. These outcomes are a neoliberal structure as their purpose is to provide a benchmark to measure student satisfaction. This is not uncommon as most universities have similar outcomes in place in order to protect the university from any legal actions (Newson, 2004). The simple idea is that if the outcomes are met, the student received what was expected, and student satisfaction is met. We recognise that the course outcomes are a required neoliberal structure and decide how we can use the structure to disrupt. The collective invites Clif to lead the work of looking at the course outcomes and revising to illustrate "a distinct identity that says who we are, what we do, and what we value" (workshop, October 2015). We work through each current course outcome, graduates of this course will demonstrate the application of knowledge and skills by:

1. being mindful, respectful and critical of the professional standards;
2. critically applying theoretical and practical knowledge, skills and dispositions of learning and teaching in early childhood and primary schools settings;
3. responding in ethical ways to diverse and changing learning and teaching contexts;
4. acting on and in accordance with democratic principles; and
5. developing dialogic and reflective practice in order to become lifelong learners.

Then we consider, what does this say about our identity—as a program, as a faculty, what we do, and what we value? What we recognize is the blandness of these statements. For the collective, they can mean anything. Some people identify these through actual assignments rather than actions and pedagogy. While others are being specific about how these might relate to action and advocacy as teachers. But what is common in the group is the lack of any commitment to anything. How can we be committed to engaging as public intellectuals without committing to anything in the early childhood teacher education program? Once we identify this gap, we are able to imagine how we might create spaces for our students to understand themselves within the world by positioning students as public intellectuals rather than consumers within the university context; paralleling our own responsibilities as academics as public intellectuals. The course outcomes then change. The early childhood/primary teacher education program will empower graduates to:

1. Foreground Aboriginal Worldviews;
2. Engage with different ways of knowing, being, and doing; and
3. Position academics and students as public intellectuals.

This shift in outcomes is not only about the content of the course, but the pedagogy and view of students. It influences policies and decision-making for our course. These outcomes illustrate the commitment to the complexity of teaching and the field. They understand the relationship between the political, ethical, and technical of teaching for both academics and pre-service teachers. These outcomes invite different ways for students and academics to make meaning in reciprocal relationships between student and academic, student and student, and pre-service teacher and children and families.

The Collective Engages with the Conceptual to Disrupt and Rethink

What we have come to realise as academics as public intellectuals is the reciprocal view that students also need to be viewed as public intellectuals. But this does not happen without the academic willing to disrupt, suggest, and rethink neoliberal structures supporting the student as consumer. This became evident in our work as a collective on college-wide working groups and in collective sessions with our early childhood faculty. This is the reasoning for including academics and students as public intellectuals in the course outcomes and for lobbying for students to be viewed as public intellectuals across the university. Academics as public intellectuals are needed to further the view of students as public intellectuals. The collective administrating and teaching into the early childhood/primary undergraduate course/program attempt to disrupt technical university structures and policy regarding class architecture.

Traditionally, the Australian higher education system utilizes the class structure of lecture/tutorial. This means students attend a lecture (usually 1 hour) and then a tutorial (typically 2 hours). The tutor leading the tutorial tends to be hired to complete a tutorial session in the morning and then the same session in the afternoon, referred to as an "original" tutorial and then a "repeat". In terms of the bottom line, this is the *most cost effective* use of hired lecturers (not staff, but part-time). Yet, this structure limits the ability for the tutors to develop any sense of relationship with the student (as every tutorial may be taught by a different part-time lecturer or sessional) or see the connection between units/class across the course/program (especially if the lecturer or sessional is teaching only one unit/class within the course/program). It becomes quite impossible for students to engage as public intellectuals within this structure.

Two units—an early childhood history and philosophy unit and a theories and practices of play in early childhood—in the first year of the early childhood/primary course became the vehicle for both academics and students to engage as public intellectuals. Considering the new course outcomes, in particular, foregrounding Aboriginal Worldviews, and engaging with different ways of knowing, being, and doing, the concepts of place-thought (Watts, 2013), learning to be affected (Latour, 2004), and past-present (King, 2004) became the concepts framing these two units. Catherine Hamm, 2015 a lecturer at Victoria University and part of the leadership team for this course and these units, notes how "place-thought pedagogies that are inclusive, respectful, and reconciled to people of the local Aboriginal group can be put to work as a decolonizing practice," exposing "layers of colonial inscription in the landscape, creating space for the land to be reclaimed and reinscribed with Aboriginal knowledges as the central frame" (p. 1). Using her paper *Walking With Place: Storying Reconciliation Pedagogies in Early Childhood Education* (2015), Hamm offers concepts that disrupt the usual dogmas of early childhood steeped in developmental psychology, cookie-cutter methods focused on literacy and maths, and plastic disconnected environments. Instead recognizing place as "alive and kicking" (Rose, 2004, p. 21); past present (King, 2004) makes visible the always entanglement of the past and present, providing "the opportunity to look deeply at the places around us, exposing the layers of inscription, acknowledging that the past still exists in the present (Hamm, 2015, p. 3); and Latour's (2004) learning to be affected is being awake to all the possibilities and proposals support a means to pay attention to "multiple ways of seeing the world around us" (Hamm, 2015, p. 4).

With the conceptual at the core of rethinking these two units, the collective then chose to resituate the units to be taught together with a tutorial in the morning, a lecture in the middle, and a second tutorial in the afternoon. Further, each student has the same lecturer/sessional for both tutorials as well as the same grouping of students. Within each tutorial, the students form learning groups that stay the same throughout the semester and across both tutorials. This sets the stage for students to develop relationships with staff/faculty and their peers in order to engage with the conceptual.

Directly tied to this experience is a placement in a family playgroup program privileging Aboriginal Worldviews and connections to place—offered 5 days over 5 weeks during the semester. Each student is placed in this program as a collaborator and support to the mentor teacher teaching the program. Two of the program sites are identified as research sites exploring specific research questions established by the staff/faculty. Students assigned to these two sites apply through an Expression of Interest and engage with research with the mentor teacher and the overseeing researcher (who is also the unit advisor and lecturer for the two units/classes described above).

When the conceptual is the priority, the technical structure then becomes the support of the conceptual. In this case, the traditional structure of the lecture-tutorial is disrupted and a class structure using small groups is put in place to encourage discussion and debate. Time is given to build relationships between academic and student as student engages with a consistent group of staff/faculty and students, creating another level of the collective. Collaboration in research between academic and students is encouraged through the placement experience and in connection to the two units/classes. The disruption of beginning with the conceptual rather than the technical shifts the usual reasoning for how classes are timetabled and delivered. Commitments to ideas and social justice (in this case, consider the course outcomes and concepts developed in this units) are paramount, pushing neoliberalism and related policy and procedures into the margin.

Disrupting the Absurd: Rethinking Structures and Policies to Support Academics as Public Intellectuals

The stories and examples we share offer ways academics are acting as public intellectuals and how the disruption and rethinking of structures and policies supports this repositioning of the academic from service provider. The overarching action of the collective of public intellectuals empowers academics to create a groundswell of voice and movement away from the considerable influence of neoliberalism on higher education contexts. Seeing disruption and rethinking in the concrete terms of structures and policies offers a real and feasible means to imagine the university outside and beyond the neoliberal order.

In our stories, we see how academics work the system of timetabling and course management to support the conceptual social-justice driven intention of the early childhood course. These actions recognise that academics still work within the neoliberal university—but are finding spaces of rethinking and resistance. Further, the technical of how units/classes are positioned and staffed supports students to engage as public intellectuals—further realisation of how both academics and students must be positioned as public intellectuals to create a university outside of commodification, market, and privatisation. The wide-awakeness and public thinking of this collective of critical early childhood teacher educators is evident in the group publications and willingness to engage with the issues of the field, regardless of the actual context of the neoliberal university and system. It is courageous to consistently continue to talk the different talk, the talk outside of what checks the boxes and drives the for-profit mentality. We see this in our examples and we are certain there are other movements and actions of academics being brave and not giving into the fatalism that neoliberalism generates.

We offer the following structures and policies as inspiration for academics to engage as public intellectuals. Each structure or policy is listed next to ways to rethink and act. This work is not about only disruption as there needs to be ways to work towards imagining what is possible beyond neoliberalism.

Ways to begin viewing academics as public intellectuals

1. *Returning back to rethinking class structures*

Relevant Policies and Structures: Timetabling, Class Size, Use of Space/ Facilities, Content/Academic Freedom

In the previous chapter focused on students as public intellectuals, we discussed rethinking the class structures in order to include spaces for discussion, debate, and disagreement. Again we return this idea for academics to engage in public intellectuals. Disrupting the usual structure of extremely large lectures (sometimes over 200 students) and large discussion/tutorial groups (at least 25 students) by rethinking policies that limit space and class size creates the possibility of activities and collaborations that complexify teaching practice and content. For example, rethinking two to three separate classes as day-long seminars constructs a framework for several different types of teaching pedagogies, groupings, and experiences to occur. Utilizing burst mode options of a unit being taught over several consistent days rather than across an entire semester of once a week also creates opportunity for unique ways for academics to engage with students and build relationships that are supportive of academics and students as public intellectuals.

As academics, the consideration of the conceptual first also changes the structures and policies that are steeped in the technical. Understanding the conceptual values driving a program will determine an academic's pedagogical choices leading to an academic's technical decisions. We see this in the example shared of the Australian early childhood course, where the course outcomes reflect the conceptual and then the pedagogies are developed to support and further these concepts. The technical is then about supporting the conceptual and pedagogical rather than the impetus for all decision-making in the program.

Questions to consider:

1. What are the conceptual ideas informing a course/program? Individual classes/units?
2. What pedagogical practices could support the introduction, exploration, and application of these conceptual ideas?
3. What are the technical structures and policies needed to support the introduction, exploration, and application of these conceptual ideas?
4. What policies and structures (the technical) already exist informing the course/program?
5. If necessary, how might these policies be revised to align with the conceptual ideas and pedagogical practices?
6. In what ways does teaching and research come together to inform each other? Are there connections between academics expertise and content in courses/programs? How are these connections seen as opportunities to connect the public with higher education?
7. Are there ways teaching and learning is reflective of both student and academic as public intellectual?

Possible actions:

1. Visually map the conceptual ideas and pedagogical practices of course/program. Visually map the policies and structures (the technical) currently supporting the program. Find the connections and disconnections. Revise any disconnections with intent of ensuring delivery of the conceptual within a course/program. Complete this process with individual classes/units.
2. Create a collaborative group of academics to review and ponder the connections between conceptual, pedagogical, and technical in teaching, research, and service across disciplines in a university. Write about discoveries, questions, and challenges through short commentaries or related works that offer provocations across higher education locally and internationally.
3. Consider ways in which research agendas create opportunities to connect teaching and learning. If possible, create ways students and academics can collaborate on research that moves beyond the higher education and engages with relevant issues in the field and community as well as apply concepts that are part of courses/programs.

2. *Rethinking teacher evaluations*

Relevant Policies and Structures: Evaluations of Teaching

Teaching evaluations continue to be a large part of the academic's university life and are often reflective of student satisfaction. Rethinking teaching evaluations beyond student satisfaction is one way to support teaching that engages academics as public intellectuals. Questions like—How did this class make

> me change my thinking? or What new ideas or perspectives were generated through this class?—present opportunities for students to share the impact of a class on their thinking and actions. Questions should be generated specifically to a class and not be generic across all classes. Further, questions should be constructed to generate qualitative response with the purpose of gathering of information that can actually improve course teaching rather than rank or judge teaching.

Questions to consider:

1. How do academics build relationships with students so feedback is more than the standardised evaluation?
2. What kind of questions can support academics in rethinking units/classes?
3. Should questions consider the conceptual, pedagogical, and technical? How might questions from each of these categories contribute to improving teaching?

Possible actions:

1. At the start of a unit/class, lead a discussion on what feedback is and what it might contribute to teaching and learning including the difference between judgement and feedback. Use these ideas as part of the class culture, create opportunities for informal and formal feedback for students.
2. Create and share questions with students that provoke thinking about the unit/class in terms of how the class, content, activities impacted the students in terms of the application of the conceptual as well as how the pedagogical and technical support this understanding.
3. Start units/classes with the following questions: How did this class make me change my thinking? What new ideas or perspectives were generated through this class? Ask students to make notes throughout the class indicating when this happened. Make visible these changes, ideas, and perspectives through on online forum or platform.
4. Write with the students about these questions or other questions generated from the start of the class as another way of understanding the impact (or lack of impact) in terms of teaching and learning.

> ### 3. *Assessment of academics*
>
> **Relevant Policies and Structures: Tenure/Promotion, Research-Related Organisation and Allocation, Publication Guidelines**
> Structure and policies related to tenure and promotion of academics can offer support of academics to engage as public intellectuals. Recognising academics that work as a collective in research, publications, and teaching in order to engage the public through related tenure and promotion policies illustrates support for academics as public intellectuals. Yet, at the same time, it creates

> safe spaces for academics to build capacity across their context, their field, and the local and global community. It opens the door for cross-disciplinary work and furthers unique collaborations between fields and unlikely participants.

Consider this scenario, a mid-career academic works with two early career academics to develop a grant application for funding for an international study tour. The purpose of the study tour is grounded in the viewing students and academics as public intellectuals, moving beyond the walls of the university in order to engage in unfamiliar contexts considering issues of social justice and teaching. The mid-career academic leads the writing of the grant application to build the capacity of these early career academics with no intent of leading the actual tour, but to engage in a support position. This decision is about building the collective, creating spaces for the early career academics to engage as public intellectuals through the conceptual, pedagogical, and technical as well as build spaces for discussion, contestation, and rethinking. Traditionally, a tenure and promotion committee might wonder why a mid-career academic would engage in this work—Does it further her research agenda? Does it further her international profile? How much money did she bring into the university? How does she and the institution benefit from this choice and time she spent engaging in this act? By rethinking assessment in a manner that is about the collective and the work of the academic as public intellectual (and in this case, the students as well), the questions the tenure and promotion committee asks are different—How did this work develop a collective in her discipline and across several disciplines? How did this academic build capacity at the institution? How are her choices in alignment with being a public intellectual?

Publications are another facet of this rethinking of assessment. Traditionally, academics are assessed on the number of publications rank of a journal, and citations. But in reality, on average only about 10 people will read one of these articles completely (Biswas & Kirchherr, 2015; O'Grady & Roos, 2016). This assessment of an academic's impact is less about how information is shared with the public towards change and more about addressing the same small academic audience, often limiting who sees and considers research and theories. By creating policies that support publication and sharing of knowledge to the general public, the academic is supported to engage as a public intellectual. This means being able to write in public spaces like newspapers, blogs, and other media and to have these publications as part of how an academic is assessed. Further, these publications often showcase the practical relevance and potential application of the research results to solve real world problems, and ability to communicate in a simple, understandable manner (Biswas & Kirchherr, 2015; http://www.straitstimes.com/opinion/prof-no-one-is-reading-you). This action of making public scholarly ideas and information offers places for debate and dialogue for all–not just those in higher education.

Questions to consider:

1. How might a collective be defined in a specific context? Are there multiple ways a collective can exist and function in higher education?
2. Can a collective include higher education and the public? Does a collective that includes higher education and the public need an issue to come together around? Or can the collective just exist as a resource? What does this kind of collective look like?
3. How do academics work to create a collective in their fields?
4. How do academics work to create a multidisciplinary collective?
5. How can academics build capacity in their university context? What resources (if any) are necessary to build capacity?
6. How can the act of publication be redefined to move beyond the academy and into the public?
7. In what ways might academics need to change their writing styles (if at all) in order to share information/knowledge/ideas with the public?
8. What policies and structures regarding publications and service exist in an institution to support connections between public and academics?
9. What informs research agendas? What policies and structures support research agendas linked to furthering humanity and social justice?

Possible actions:

1. Create opportunities for academics to create collectives focused on real issues in the field. This could include responding to events in local and global communities.
2. Review tenure and/or promotion policies to see where academics are supported to form collectives, work with the public, and ensure expertise is shared in ways that the public is further empowered.
3. Review how scholarship and service are defined in the context of a university. If scholarship and service are only related to career advancement, revise these definitions so they are situated in humanity and equity across the university and beyond. Discuss how these foundational understandings might rethink other related policies and structures.
4. Create research hubs in the community in places like schools or community centres (places where your research is relevant) where the public can be part of the research. If possible, create a cohort of post-graduate students in the research hub, creating learning experiences with and in the community.

References

AAUP. (2015). Teaching evaluations survey.
Adkins, A., Spesia, T., & Snakenborg, J. (2015). Rebuttal to Dover et al. *Teachers College Record*.
Agius, K., Aitken, J., Blaise, M., Boucher, K., Hamm, C., Iorio, J. M., ... McCartin, J. (2015a). Who's swallowing the *Action Now: Classroom Ready Teachers* report?: Discussing, understanding, and

References

wondering. *Teacher College Record*, ID Number: 17971. Retrieved from February 18, 2015, from http://www.tcrecord.org.

Agius, K., Aitken, J., Blaise, M., Boucher, K. Hamm, C., Iorio, J. M., ... Nehma, N. (2015b). Critically imagining an early childhood 'classroom ready' teacher. *Professional Educator*.

Aronowitz, S. (2000). *The knowledge factory: Dismantling the corporate university and creating true higher learning*. Boston: Beacon Press.

Axelrod, Y., Black, F., Cheruvu, R., Murphy, A.M., Pérez, M.S., Rabadi-Raol, A., Rollins, E., & Saavedra, C.M. (2018). Representation of people of color in critical early childhood spaces: Issues and possibilities. *Teachers College Record*.

Biswas, A., & Kirchherr, J. (2015). Prof, no one is reading you. *The Strait Times*. Retrieved from https://www.straitstimes.com/opinion/prof-no-one-is-reading-you.

Blaise, M., Hamm, C., & Iorio, J.M. (2016). Modest witness(ing): Paying attention to matters of concern in early childhood. *Pedagogy, Culture, and Society*.

Boring, A., Ottoboni, K., & Stark, P. (2016). Student evaluations of teaching (mostly) do not measure teacher effectiveness. *ScienceOpen research*, 1–11, https://doi.org/10.14293/s2199-1006.1.sor-edu.aetbzc.vl.

Bromell, N. (2002). Summa Cum Avaritia: Plucking profit from the Groves of Academe. *Harper's Magazine*, 71–76 (2002).

Burns, J. (2016). Where do I fit in? Adrift in neoliberal educational anti-culture. *Teachers College Record*. Retrieved from http://www.tcrecord.org/Content.asp?ContentID=20275.

Conley, M., & Garner, G. (2015). The edTPA and The (De)Skilling of America's Teachers? *Teachers College Record*. Retrieved July 17, 2015, from http://www.tcrecord.org. ID Number: 18037, Date Accessed July 10, 2018, 6:07:47 AM.

Cote, Day, & de Peuter. (2007). Utopian pedagogy: Creating radical alternatives in the neoliberal age. *Review of Education, Pedagogy, and Cultural Studies, 29*(4), 317–336.

CReATE. (2015). *Chicago school reform: Myths, realities, and new visions*. Retrieved from http://www.createchicago.org/.

Dahlberg, G., Moss, P., & Pence, A. (2007). Beyond quality in early childhood education and care: A postmodern perspective. London and New York: Routledge/Falmer.

Dover, A., Schultz, B., Smith, K., & Duggan, T. (2015a). Embracing the controversy: edTPA, Corporate Influence, and the Cooptation of Teacher Education. *Teachers College Record*. Retrieved September 14, 2015, from http://www.tcrecord.org. ID Number: 18109, Date Accessed July 10, 2018, 6:01:58 AM.

Dover, A., Schultz, B., Smith, K., & Duggan, T. (2015b). Who's preparing our candidates? edTPA, Localized knowledge and the outsourcing of teacher evaluation. *Teachers College Record*, Retrieved March 30, 2015, from http://www.tcrecord.org. ID Number: 17914, Date Accessed July 10, 2018, 6:05:44 AM.

Dryden-Peterson, S. (2016). Refugee education: The crossroads of globalization. *Educational Researcher, 45*(9), 473–482.

Edmundson, M. (1997, September). On the uses of a liberal education: Part 1—As light entertainment for bored college students. *Harper's Magazine*, 39–49.

Edwards, C., Gandini, L., & Forman, G. (Eds.). (1998). The hundred languages of children: The Reggio Emilia approach: Advanced reflections. Westport, CT: Ablex.

Flaherty, C. (2016, June 10). Flawed evaluations. *Inside Higher Education*.

Fraser, H., & Taylor, N. (2016). *Neoliberalization, Universities and the Public Intellectual*. New York: Palgrave.

Garlen, J., Kuh, L., & Coleman, B. (2017). Teaching for social justice in the early childhood classroom. *Teachers College Record*. Retrieved March 27, 2017, from http://www.tcrecord.org. ID Number: 21890, Date Accessed July 10, 2018, 6:16:40 AM.

Giroux, H. (2013/2014). Public intellectuals against the neo-liberal university. In N. K. Denzin & M. Giardina (Eds.), *Qualitative inquiry outside the academy* (pp. 35–60). Walnut Creek, CA: Left Coast Press.

Greene, M. (1978). *Landscapes on learning*. New York: Teachers College Press.

Greene, M. (1995). *Releasing the imagination: Essays on education, the arts, and social change*. San Francisco: Jossey-Bass.
Greene, M. (2000). The ambiguities of freedom. *English Education, 33*, 8–14.
Greene, M. (2005). Teaching in a moment of crisis: The spaces of imagination. *The New Educator, 1*, 77–80.
Greene, M. (2012). *Inside the academy: Maxine Greene*. Retrieved from https://www.youtube.com/watch?v=R8hp8GD8-p4.
Hamm, C. (2015). Walking with place: Storying reconciliation pedagogies in early childhood education. *Canadian Children, 40*(2), 57–67. The Canadian Association for Young Children.
Hamm, C., & Boucher, K. (2018). Engaging with place: Foregrounding aboriginal perspective in early childhood education. In N. Yelland & D. Bentley (Eds.), *Found in translation: Connecting reconceptualist early childhood ideas with practice*. New York: Routledge.
Hamm, C., Nehma, N., McCartin, J., Lovell, B., Iorio, J.M., Boucher, K., ... Agius, K. (2017). Engaging with ethical resistance and courageous activism: A response to where do I fit in? Adrift in neoliberal educational anti-culture. *Teachers College Record*. Retrieved January 9, 2017.
Haraway, D. J. (2008). *When species meet*. Minneapolis: University of Minnesota Press.
Hill, (2016). The conference: An overview and assessment. *Australian Universities Review, 58*(2), 5–8.
Holzer, H. (2015). *Higher education and workforce policy: Creating more skilled workers (and jobs for them to fill)*. Economic studies at Brookings, Brookings Institution, Washington, Retrieved July 9, 2018, from <http://www.brookings.edu/research/papers/2015/04/higher-ed-workforce-policy-skilled-workers-holzer>.
Iorio, J. M., Hamm, C., Parnell, W., & Quintero, E. (2017). Place, matters of concern, and pedagogy: Making impactful connections with our planet. *Journal of Early Childhood Teacher Education, 32*(2), 121–135. https://doi.org/10.1080/10901027.2017.1306600.
Iorio, J. M., Coustley, A., & Grayland, (2018). Practicing pedagogical documentation: Teachers making more-than-human relationships and sense of place visible. In N. Yelland & D. Bentley (Eds.), *Found in translation: Connecting reconceptualist early childhood ideas with practice*. New York: Routledge.
Jakobi, M. (2016). A stab in the dark: Anonymous student evaluations of Aboriginal Teacher Educators. *Teachers College Record*. Retrieved September 21, 2016, from http://www.tcrecord.org. ID Number: 21653.
Jordan, A., & Hawley, T. (2016). By the Elite, For the Vulnerable: The edTPA, Academic Oppression, and the Battle to Define Good Teaching. *Teachers College Record*.
King, K. (2004). Historiography as reenactment: Metaphors and literalizations of TV documentaries. *Criticism, 46*(3), 459–475.
Latour, B. (2004). How to talk about the body? The normative dimension of science studies. *Body & society, 10*(2--3), 205--229.
Latour, B. (2005). *Reassembling the social: An introduction to Actor-Network-Theory*. New York, NY: Oxford University Press.
Lester, S., & Costley, (2010). Work-based learning at higher education level: Value, practice and critique. *Studies in Higher Education, 35*(5), 561–575. https://doi.org/10.1080/03075070903216635.
Levy, B., Solomon, B., & Collet-Gildard, L. (2016). Fostering political interest among youth during the 2012 presidential election: Instructional opportunities and challenges in a swing state. *Educational Researcher, 45*(9), 483–495.
MacNell, L., Driscoll, A., & Hunt, A. N. (2015). What's in a name: Exposing gender bias in student ratings of teaching. *Innovative Higher Education, 40*(4), 291–303.
Moss, P. (2016). Why can't we get beyond quality. *Contemporary Issues in Early Childhood Education, 17*(1), 8–15.
Newson, J. A. (2004). Disrupting the 'student as consumer' model: The new emancipatory project. *International Relations, 18*(2), 227–229.

References

O'Grady, K. & Roos, N. (2016). It's time for a global movement that pushes academic research beyond journal paywalls so it makes a difference in the world. *Policy Options*. Retrieved from http://policyoptions.irpp.org/magazines/august-2016/linking-academic-research-with-the-public-and-policy-makers/.

Parnell, W. (2011). Revealing the experience of children and teachers even in their absence: Documenting in the early childhood studio. *Journal of Early Childhood Research, 9*(3), 291–309. Retrieved from https://doi.org/10.1177/1476718x10397903.

Peters, L., Reinke, S., & Castner, D. (2017). Critically engaging in discourses on quality improvement: Political and pedagogical futures in early childhood education. *Teachers College Record*. Retrieved from June 27, 2017, from http://www.tcrecord.org. ID Number: 22063, Date Accessed July 10, 2018, 6:12:56 AM.

Phillips, S. (2016). Don't read the comments! *Agenda, 24,* 17.

Pinar, W. (2012). *What is curriculum theory?* New York: Routledge.

Pink, S. (2008, June). An urban tour: The sensory sociality of ethnographic place-making. *Ethnography, 9,* 175–196. https://doi.org/10.1177/1466138108089467.

Rose, D. B. (2004). Reports from a wild country: Ethics for decolonisation. Sydney, Australia: University of New South Wales Press.

Quintero, E. P. (2009). *Refugee and immigrant family voices: Experience and education*. The Netherlands: Sense Publishers.

Quintero, E. P. (2011). Quality early care and education: Collaborating for children of agricultural workers, *Bridges*. Sacramento, CA: California Head Start—State Collaboration Office.

Quintero, E. P. (2017). Carrying our Roots/llevar a nuestras raíces. Special Issue: *Rethinking global north onto-epistemologies in childhood studies* for the *Global Studies of Childhood (GSC)*.

Quintero, E. P., & Rummel, M. K. (2014). *Storying, a path to our future: Artful thinking, learning, teaching, and research*. New York: Peter Lang, Series on Critical Perspectives in Qualitative Research.

Rinaldi, C. (2006). *In dialogue with Reggio Emilia: Listening, researching and learning*. Abingdon, UK: Routledge.

Said, E. (1996). *Representations of the intellectual: The 1993 Reith lectures*. New York: Vintage.

Saunders, D. (2011). Neoliberal ideology and public higher education in the United States. *Journal for Critical Education Policy Studies, 8*(1), 41–77.

Schmidt, B. (2015). *Gendered language in teacher reviews*. http://benschmidt.org/.

Schuman, R. (2014). Needs improvement. *Slate*. Retrieved April 24, 2014, from http://www.slate.com/news-and-politics/2018/07/epa-administrator-scott-pruitts-sloppy-corrupt-attack-on-the-environment-backfired.html.

Slaughter, S., & Rhoades, G. (2004). *Academic capitalism and the new economy: Markets, state, and higher education*. Baltimore, MD: John Hopkins University Press.

Solomon, S., Plattner, G.-K., Knutti, R., & Friedlingstein, P. (2009). Irreversible climate change due to carbon dioxide emissions. *Proceedings of the National Academy of Sciences, 106,* 1704–1709. https://doi.org/10.1073/pnas.0812721106.

Soslau, E., Kotch-Jester, S., Jortin, A. (2015). The dangerous message teacher candidates infer: "If the edTPA Does Not Assess It, I Don't Have to Do It". *Teachers College Record*. Retrieved December 11, 2015, from http://www.tcrecord.org. ID Number: 18835, Date Accessed July 10, 2018, 5:58:05 AM.

Stark, P. (2014). An evaluation of course evaluations. *ScienceOpen Researcher*, 1–26. https://doi.org/10.14293/s2199-1006.1.sor-edu.aofrqa.v1.

Taylor, A., & Guigini, M. (2012). Common worlds: Reconceptualising inclusion in early childhood communities. *Contemporary Issues in Early Childhood, 13*(2), 2012.

Taylor, A., & Pacini-Ketchabaw, V. (2015). Learning with children, ants, and worms in the anthropocene: Towards a common world pedagogy of multispecies vulnerability. *Pedagogy, Culture & Society, 23*(4), 507–529.

Teacher Education Ministerial Advisory Group (TEMAG). (2014). *Action now: Classroom ready teachers*. Canberra, Australia: Australian Government Department of Education & Training. Retrieved from http://docs.education.gov.au/system/files/doc/other/action_now_classroom_ready_teachers_accessible.pdf.

Tuck, E., McKenzie, M., & McCoy, M. (2014). Land education: Indigenous, post-colonial, and decolonizing perspectives on place and environmental education research. *Environmental Education Research, 20*(1), 1–23. https://doi.org/10.1080/13504622.2013.877708.

Victoria State Government Department of Education and Training. (2016, August). Working together to shape teacher education in Victoria: Discussion paper. Melbourne, AU. Author. Retrieved from http://www.education.vic.gov.au/Documents/workingtogether.pdf.

Watts, V. (2013). "Indigenous place-thought and agency amongst humans and non humans (First Woman and Sky Woman go on a European world tour!)" decolonization: Indigeneity. *Education & Society, 2*(1), 20–34.

Chapter 5
Administrator as Public Intellectual

A very worthy person, an administrator, and whose virtues we highly esteem, is another cog in this neoliberal machine. As the manager of the institute of higher education discoursing on this matter to offer refinement upon our scheme. His position of supporting the thinking student and academic will be conceived that the want of thinking will be well supplied under the guise of managerialism. This will dispose of thinking as students and academics will be tricked into the engaging with the "process" but of reality, the thinking will be ignored as decisions are already made in the name of profit and bottom-line.

The absurd: *His position of supporting the thinking student and academic will be conceived that the want of thinking will be well supplied under the guise of managerialism. This will dispose of thinking as students and academics will be tricked into the engaging with the "process" but of reality, the thinking will be ignored as decisions are already made in the name of profit and bottom-line.*

Clif always wanted to be a professor. And so he starts his career as a professor. On his first day at a new university, he walks onto campus and enters into the usual ritual–the tour by the chair of the department. Walking on the paths, down the halls, the pointing of where this is, where that is. Clif begins to be called into connection to the place. And then the chair stops and points to Clif's new office. Connection made! This is the space in this place that names him as part of the community. The door is ajar. Slowly it opens. Inside another person is putting things in a box. His body moving in chorus to a staccato composition of music that no one can hear. Pick up a book; Put it in the box; Pick up a book; Put it in the box; Pick up a book; Put it in the box. And then the movements stop as eyes lock. Brief introductions are made, then words travel directly to Clif, You do know that you were the affirmative action candidate. There were other more qualified applicants.

Clif glanced awkwardly at the chair. Silence.

Disconnection from place, from community. Clif turns and walks out of the space, out of the building, off the campus, back to his home. Only one line running through his head, I must get out of this job. I have to leave this place.

The phone rings, inside Clif's home, a place where he is connected and welcomed, he answers. The dean of the college is on the other end. Words come through the receiver—I heard what happened. Will you come and see me in the morning? Clif agrees but still running through this head, I must get out of this job. I have to leave this place.

In the morning, before seeing the Dean, Clif finds a letter in his college inbox. It is from the dean and copied to Clif—not directed to Clif but to the person responsible for creating the disconnect, the one that made those words public, You do know that you were the affirmative action candidate. There were other more qualified candidates. The tone of the letter is direct, I want to clarify for you, in no uncertain terms, that Clif was hired because he was the most qualified applicant in the search.

This was Clif's initiation into the academy. As his experience grew, this initiation began to crystallize and tippify for Clif what ethical leadership looks like. It engages. It is direct. It does not hide or equivocate. It seeks what is good for the organization by fostering productive relationships and commitment to mission through ethical decision making.

Later that day, the Dean also made clear to Clif, how the decision was made to hire him. We have limited resources at our university and we are very careful with them. We do not take hiring decisions lightly. We conducted a careful search for this position and you are clearly the most qualified candidate for this position. He wants Clif to understand that this situation should never have happened. You, Clif, are the one we want for this job. Clif begins to build a connection to this place again. Ethical leadership action has created a space for Clif's work as a public intellectual.

Hope and Resistance to Neoliberalism

We offer this story first for a reason. This story for us is the practice of hope—an administrator as public intellectual. Regardless of the context of this university and the implications of neoliberalism, this administrator makes a choice towards humanity disrupting the expecting management level decisions steeped in bottom line with relationships in the margin, if anywhere at all. In this interaction, hope exists. While hope of place may have been challenged first during Clif's campus tour, hope is restored as the administrator engages completely with the situation. He does not hide and push this moment off as something small, unimportant. His actions create this university as a guide for hope, a place for humans to engage in the search for hope. This connection, this commitment, this choice is resistance to neoliberalism in higher education because the administrator engages in relationship building—it is not a vacant process of faux listening so often demonstrated when administrators name themselves as managers. Rather, it is a messy, honest, and in moments, a shared power dynamic between academic and administrator. It redefines the administrator as public intellectual as the administrator disrupts and resists management practices steeped in control and power, and rethinks how an administrator can be imagined in higher education. In this sense, the administrator as public intellectual is different than the student and academic as public intellectual. For the administrator, engaging as a public intellectual is about creating spaces and supports for students and academics to act as public intellectuals.

Another Story

An invitation is received by an academic, The Dean and Associate Dean invite you to be part of working group contributing to a new vision of innovation for the college and implementation of programs across the college under this new vision. How exciting to be able to contribute to the possibilities of what will happen next in the university! Meetings begin, one every week for over a month. A group of academics representative of programs throughout the college; all excited to ponder and offer concrete ways to move forward, towards the new vision. A question is posed by one of the academics, a female in the group, what is the underlying view of the student we are considering? Are we viewing the student as consumer? Or a capable, competent, and contributing person? The Associate Dean avoids the question and says both. Academics in the group push him for an answer. A tensions emerges. This continues to be a heated discussion across the group. About half-way through the third meeting, the female academic brings it up again in another discussion around the non-traditional population the university is serving and whether the student as consumer really responds to the need of these students. She begins to cite some examples and abruptly stops and looks directly at the Associate Dean sitting next to her. "Did you mean to kick me?" Yes, while she is sharing her ideas, he kicks her in the shin. "Yes, I want you to stop talking about that."

This story represents something other than hope—a narrow view that higher education is about money and bottom-lines and that no matter what, the administrator functions always believing the student as consumer. This is important enough to silence an academic questioning the view. This is not surprising as New Public Management (NPM) approaches continue to dominate universities (Fraser & Taylor, 2016; Lorenz, 2012). According to Lorenz (2012), NPM:

1. is a combination of free market rhetoric and intensive managerial control practices;
2. employs a discourse that parasitizes the everyday meanings of their concepts—efficiency, accountability, transparency, and (preferably excellent) quality—and simultaneously perverts all their original meanings; and

3. ignores the most important aspects of the education process and therefore poses a fundamental threat to education itself.
(p. 600)

In the story shared above, we witness the use of both "free market rhetoric" as student as consumer and "intensive managerial control practices" as the Associate Dean chooses to silence the academic by a kick. We see how the word innovation far from its original definition and ideas are "innovative" when they ensure the bottom-line and customer satisfaction. And finally, we note how the idea of creating and implementing programs where students are seen as capable, competent, and contributing people to local and global communities is ignored and view of the student as consumer is primary. The hope for humanity is not in this session—but neoliberalism is—and it is further perpetuated by an overzealous administrator with only one intention, ensuring the continuation of control in name of profit. "The aim, it seems, is to produce docile students without critical thinking abilities, who are fully enrolled in ideological notions of individuality and personal success, irrespective of and largely blind to any social costs this entails" (Fraser & Taylor, 2016, p. 5).

The management techniques employed by the administrator in the story above compel academics and staff "to behave in ways we neither like nor would freely choose" (Fraser & Taylor, 2016, p. 6). If we continue the story above, we would find out that the male administrator was never penalised by the university for his behaviour, even after the female academic shared her experience with human resources. We also would hear how the female academic is well-aware of how her "telling" would be perceived as someone that just has not "embraced the marketization of the academy", often critical and resisting (p. 6). There is no space for her to act as public intellectual. This administrator is not a public intellectual and he has ensured there is not space for any public intellectuals to exist—fellow administrators, academics, or students.

This is the administrator as manager—sometimes even labeled the CEO—situating profit, capitalism, and market at the center of decision-making and purposes like the common good are no longer part of university responsibilities. Terms like managerialism, NPM, and managerial technologies flood the position description of an administrator in higher education. But how did we get here?

Higher Education Administrator as Manager

Traditionally, higher education appealed to principles of shared governance, collaboration, and mutual commitment, and where, ideally, the faculty and the administration are aligned regarding the direction of the institution as they work to set institutional policy and direction (Bahls, 2014). However, higher education today has begun to incorporate a different set of principles that have repositioned the administrator as manager. "A necessary condition of the managerial model was the elimination of any semblance of collegial democracy. The self-governing faculty has been replaced by a hierarchy of managers empowered to direct and instruct their subordinates" (West, 2015). These ideas contribute to the reframing of the university to

> what Bill Readings has called "the university of excellence." The vice-chancellor, deans and heads of department have increasingly become "knowledge managers" in a knowledge corporation charged with running the university through a strategic planning process in accordance with targets, new incentive structures, and policy directives at the expense of traditional collegial and democratic governance.
> (Peters, Liu, & Ondercin, 2012, p. 93)

Managers, corporation, incentives, and the disappearance of democracy (and the rise of administrators kicking academics and staff literally and metaphorically) all reflective the practice of managerialism.

Managerialism

Following the postwar reconstruction economy of the 1970s, managerialism as a concept and approach has taken hold in both for profit and nonprofit sectors (like higher education) (Doran, 2016). While few theorist have offered explicit definitions of the concept, Enteman (1993) posits that a basic assumption of managerialism is that the fundamental social unit is the organization, not the individual, nor the state. A managerialist society is not based on democratic ideals, and does not operate according to "the needs, desires and wishes of a majority of its citizens" (p. 154).

Economist Quiggin (2003) argues that the "central doctrine of managerialism is that the differences between such organizations as, for example, a university and a motor-vehicle company, are less important than the similarities, and that the performance of all organizations can be optimised by the application of generic management skills and theory" (Retrieved from http://johnquiggin.com/2003/07/02/word-for-wednesday-managerialism-definition). He goes on to suggest that a key feature of managerialism is a focus on optimizing policy and rejecting professionalism. Rather than maximising worker skill and expertise, managerialist organizations apply universal management techniques, such as; organizational restructuring, increasing incentives, raising the profile of senior managers and downgrading the role of skilled workers and professionals.

Managerialism and Higher Education

Santiago and Carvalho (2004) identify four key elements of managerialism in higher education including the:

- separation between teaching and research as a way to increase their efficiency and productivity;
- development of 'entrepreneurial research' or 'strategic research', oriented towards knowledge transfer and technological innovation in companies;

- replacement of higher education's traditional sociocultural goals, inherited from the welfare state, by utilitarian ones; and
- submission of curricula design to labour market requirements.

(p. 433).

Orr and Orr (2016) define managerialism as "through the use of bureaucratic procedures and metrics, the activities of individuals and groups should be controlled by individuals not performing such activities. This is often believed to increase efficiency."

(p. 16)

Both of these definitions indicate a high level of control and structure in the name of efficiency. Interestingly, managerialism is a consequence of neoliberalism which heralds "unregulated market to optimise human relations" (Orr & Orr, 2016, p. 15). Yet, managerialism continues to prevail even in this inconsistency. In a research study of two universities—one non-managerial university and one managerial university, Orr and Orr (2016) look at practices and procedures to understand the impact of managerialism including creating course profile/syllabus, creation of exam, and tutor/teaching assistant contracts per tutor, per class. The following diagrams indicate the data from this research (Figs. 5.1, 5.2 and 5.3) (on the left is the managerial university; on the right is the non-managerial university).

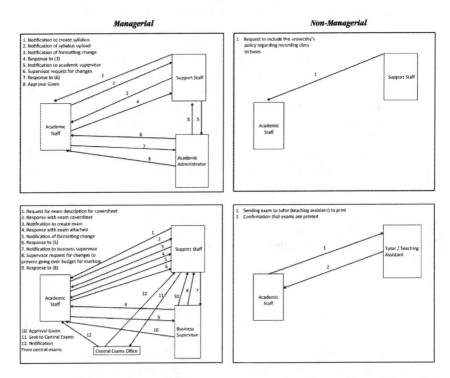

Fig. 5.1 Creation of course profile/syllabus (with permission from Raymond Orr and Yancey Orr)

Managerialism and Higher Education

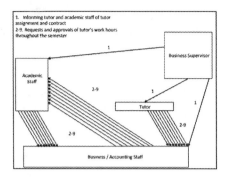 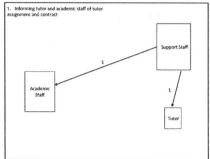

Fig. 5.2 Tutor/teaching assistant contracts per-tutor, per-class (with permission from Raymond Orr and Yancey Orr)

The diagrams are quite powerful as they indicate the massive amount of administration, red tape, and management managerialism has generated in the expected tasks in higher education. In a system with the goal of efficiency, managerial techniques seem to fail. Further, managerialism produces a tremendous amount of work with "little positive influence on the learning, research, and quality of the education institutions or the lives of those working in them."

(Orr & Orr, 2016, p. 21)

If managerialism has this large of a hold on higher education, is it even possible for administrators to engage as public intellectuals or to create spaces for students and academics to be public intellectuals? We contend that yes, even in the narrow role neoliberalism has created in higher education, there are ways administrators can be/become wide-awake and practice hope towards humanity.

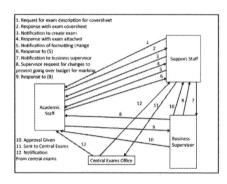 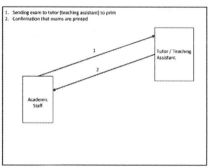

Fig. 5.3 Creation of exam (with permission from Raymond Orr and Yancey Orr)

Disrupting the Absurd: Rethinking the Administrator as Public Intellectual

Through the practice of hope, we rethink the administrator as public intellectual. This rethinking disrupts and rethinks the administrator as manager. It sees the administrator as creating spaces within higher education to act as public intellectual and create and support students and academics as public intellectuals.

There are administrators already doing this work. For example, President Michael M. Crow from Arizona State University utilises the eight design aspirations for a "A New American University" as a means to the meet the objective of preparing thought-leaders "focused on deriving purpose-driven solutions and improving the quality of life for all mankind" (https://newamericanuniversity.asu.edu/about/new-objective). The design aspirations include:

1. Leverage Our Place: ASU embraces its cultural, socioeconomic and physical setting.
2. Transform Society: ASU catalyzes social change by being connected to social needs.
3. Value Entrepreneurship: ASU uses its knowledge and encourages innovation.
4. Conduct Use-Inspired Research: ASU research has purpose and impact.
5. Enable Student Success: ASU is committed to the success of each unique student.
6. Fuse Intellectual Disciplines: ASU creates knowledge by transcending academic disciplines.
7. Be Socially Embedded: ASU connects with communities through mutually beneficial partnerships.
8. Engage Globally: ASU engages with people and issues locally, nationally and internationally.

Across the objective and the design aspirations is the connection between higher education and communities beyond the university. These are the policies and structures in place to ensure students, academics, and administrators can engage as public intellectuals.

This is further evident in the following descriptions where administrators are imagining what can possible in higher education beyond neoliberalism.

What we do realise that in this chapter is that female leadership is not represented. During our conversations with administrators, we did speak with Elizabeth Quintero and Beth Blue Swadener. The work of Elizabeth Quintero is located in Chaps. 3 and 4 in the text while Beth's work is featured in Chap. 6 and refers to some of their work as administrators in their contexts.

Story 1: Young Administrators, Leadership, and the Public Good

Clif always an advocate, often in dialogue with the public about relevant issues. He writes legislative testimony and editorials, researches towards social justice, organises and leads public debates. It is fitting that as a young administrator, Clif takes on the directorship for a faculty leadership development program. The intention of this program is creating opportunities, new spaces, and innovative frameworks for early and mid-career academics to move into leadership roles across the university. Donor-funded, the program is not a line-item in the budget, and now the program is in trouble. Clif is asked to try and save it.

Clif begins by asking current participants to think with him—What might be the core principles, dispositions, and aspects of university leadership? How do we make these ideas visible within the university and beyond?

The conversation begins. And then something interesting and not surprising to Clif materialises. We as academic leaders have a commitment, no, an obligation to work towards the interests of society. This powerful statement penetrates the group, shifting from a beginning conversation to a conceptual foundation to action–the Community Give Back Project emerges.

Situated as integrated public engagement, university expertise, and scholarship moves into the realm of service. The first project comes to fruition addressing school improvement. Through public forums and debates, information is shared. The public and the university come together to share knowledge, experiences, and challenges. This is how policy is informed and impacted.

Story 2: Administrator Making Spaces for Students and Academics as Public Intellectuals

So what happens when an administrator leads a graduate school that has established structures and policies supportive of academics and students engaging as public intellectuals?

The SelfDesign Institute (SDGI) (located in the state of Washington, USA) and David Marshak, founding President and former Academic Dean, illustrate a powerful example of the administrator as public intellectual. While David outrightly states that as an administrator, there really is no "public" or "governmental" audience, we would argue that his work as administrator is about supporting and creating spaces for both academics and students to engage as public intellectuals. His contributions in co-creating and implementing the programs at SDGI articulate the connections between vision, policy, and practice necessary to create working and evolving spaces for all stakeholders to engage as public intellectuals.

In his previous position as a Professor at Seattle University for 14 years, David "intentionally enacted the role of the public intellectual" (personal email, 2017). This included writing op-ed columns for the *Seattle Times* and the *Seattle Public-Intelligencer*, being a "regular source" for local education reporters, and appearing on public radio and televisions programs. Further examples of David's engagement with the public consisted of regular participation and lectures for the public, consulting with elected and appointed government officials, contributing to writing legislation, and testifying regarding both city and state legislation. As a member of a council gathering advocates for civil rights, David was consistently in dialogue across the Latino, African–American, Asian–American, and Pacific Islander communities as well as leaders from the Somali and Eritrean immigrant communities. These experiences inform his current work as an administrator and influence the creation and structures of SDGI.

SDGI is grounded in the understanding that all learners are capable of the "authoring of her/his own learning and life within a learning community" (SDGI Learner Handbook, 2018, p. 5). Created by a group of educators including Brent Cameron Ph.D., University of British Columbia; David Marshak Ed. D., Harvard University; Pille Bunnell Ph.D., University of California, Berkeley; Elaine Decker Ph.D., University of British Columbia; Fleurette Sweeney Ph.D., University of British Columbia; Kathleen Forsythe and Darrell Letourneau, M.A., University of Victoria, SDGI uses the structures of low-residency and distance education. SDGI offers Masters level degrees focused on SelfDesign. These programs support "learners to use their M.A. program in SelfDesign as a vehicle for shaping their lives in ways that both promote their own satisfaction, well-being and happiness and offer meaningful service to others" (p. 5). According to the SDGI Self-Evaluation Report (2017),

SelfDesign as an educational philosophy and praxis draws on the work of Francis Parker, John Dewey, Maria Montessori, Rudolf Steiner, A. S. Neill, Carl Rogers, John P. Miller and many others. This philosophy and praxis is detailed today in the extensive theory and research of Edward L. Deci and Richard M. Ryan and their many colleagues in Self-Determination Theory (http://selfdeterminationtheory.org/). Our core value is an understanding that learners of every age have the capacity to lead their own learning. SelfDesign starts from this assertion of the "freedom to learn," as Rogers called it, and adds significant contemporary elements to the learning paradigm from cognitive, developmental, humanistic, and transpersonal psychology, from research on mentoring, and from consciousness studies, evolutionary theory, and brain science. Self-Determination theory works with an organismic dialectical approach. It begins with the assumption that people are active organisms, with evolved tendencies toward growing, mastering ambient challenges, and integrating new experiences into a coherent sense of self. These natural developmental tendencies do not, however, operate automatically, but instead require ongoing social nutriments and supports. That is, the social context can support or thwart the natural tendencies toward active engagement and psychological growth, or it can catalyze lack of integration, defense, and fulfillment of need-substitutes. Thus, it is the dialectic between the active organism and the social context that is the basis for Self-Determination Theory's predictions about behavior, experience, and development (Deci, Ryan, & Guay, 2013).

(p. 7)

Founder Brent Cameron articulates the foundational perspectives of SelfDesign in the Learner Handbook and Catalog (2018),

> SelfDesign is centered on the understanding that we as human beings have the capacity to author our own lives from a place of resourcefulness, creativity, and possibility. At every

step in the life cycle from early childhood to elderhood, we can lead and design our own learning through spirals of discovery, introspection, integration, and expression.

SelfDesign is a new paradigm of learning, a new way of thinking about learning beyond schooling. It is a modern educational methodology in alignment with ancient insights and perennial truths. It blends together the masculine and the feminine, the east and the west, allowing the infinite wisdom within to play a role in healing our universe. A new world view is possible when each one of us is allowed to be free—free to choose to work within nature and natural systems, and free to live as an expression of our heart. SelfDesign is about living in enthusiasm.

(https://selfdesigninstitute.org/wp-content/uploads/2018/01/2018Learner-HandbookVol.1.pdf)

These outcomes for the graduates of SDGI reflect a disruption of the student as consumer and academic as service provider as they situate learning in self-discovery and engagement of the "whole" person in regard not only to self but connected to the local and global community. This connection beyond self, within a group, and participant in the world harks back to Greene's (1995) notion of "wide-awakeness"—"awareness of what it is to be in the world" (p. 35)—as application of their education to their lives and impact on the world is clearly articulated.

- To nurture our learners as they gain greater access both to their inner knowing and their insight about how they want to selfdesign their Master of Arts program and their lives;
- To provide each learner with an ecology of foundational insights, understandings, and skills through our Core courses, with a focus on SelfDesign, epistemology, ontology, systems concepts, and learning in community;
- To engage our learners in rigorous and challenging academic work that supports the learning plans they have selfdesigned and to provide careful mentoring through this process;
- To engage our learners deeply as whole persons—body, heart, mind, and soul—as they selfdesign and engage in their M.A. program; and
- To support our learners as they use the knowledge, wisdom, and tools they gain in their M.A. program to make a positive difference in their world.

While the outcomes are focused on the actions of the learner, the implication for the academic with these stated outcomes is support for an academic that thinks beyond the university walls and considers education as a means of disruption. This is an expected practice in these higher education classrooms. But these objectives are not just abstract—they are fully implemented in the practical daily life of SDGI. For example, as students complete 36 semester credits to earn their degree, they design over 65% of their program through electives, directed studies, and a thesis/project. The choice of structure that situates the learner as capable of choosing her or his own path further implies an established image of the student (learner in this context) as competent and capable. A structure does not exist for the learner to step into; rather the structure is flexible and evolves based on the learner as an active participant. Reading, reflection, and self-assessment are part of the pedagogy as well as small group conversations and one-on-one meetings with faculty. An important structure of the programs is the "low residency workshop" model. Through two 8-day residency workshops, learners meet with colleagues and with faculty mentors daily. This is integrated with both synchronous and asynchronous experiences constructed by elective classes and directed studies. Individual discussions as well as small groups are utilised as a means to engage with the content, connecting to personal experiences and understanding the relevance in the larger world. Through these practices, relationships between academics and students are key as both academics and students are given the space to question, think, and reflect.

Story 3: Administrator Making Space to Move Beyond the University

A strategic opportunity to make a difference—this statement rings through the air at a crowded restaurant as we sit and discuss the administrator as public intellectual with Professor William Gaudelli, the chair of large department within a graduate school of education. The strategic opportunity he is referring to is his own position on the Board of Education in his community. This is only one example of how this administrator is a public intellectual. For this administrator and member of the Board of Education, the translation of scholarship and evidence created in higher education to is shared with the public in manner a which can be understood and used is critical to how he engages as public intellectual. He know that bridging the gap between the scholarly world and the community is a value he holds as an administrator. This becomes more evident as he describes some of his projects—working with international communities to solve problems by finding design solutions with children, leading professional development of teachers in relation to global competency in order to support students as citizens of local and global community, and creating leadership curriculum for international contexts of junior high and high school students. His work is constant and always towards the public good.

He knows that this work is against the elite and complex construct of the university and states how we need to challenge this—moving toward a "new" university where the gist of what scholars say is translated to the public and into the doing. Administration and leadership need to resource this move where the university is part of the public sphere—where intent of the higher education is going beyond university walls. The university is a powerful platform for public work and it is in this view of higher education that the administrator, student, and academic can thrive as public intellectuals. Public intellectuals require the ability to connect, to be humble, to understand where others are in the world and the community. He moves on to tell us a powerful example of how this is done. As part of his budget as an administrator, he allots monies for faculty members to work with public schools on real projects with real need. This is a voluntary project that any faculty member may participate in—but overall, he creates a space for academics to reach people and community with real support.

Disrupting the Absurd: Rethinking Structures and Policies to Support Administrators as Public Intellectuals

There is a common thread across all three descriptions of these administrators and their work—they come to administration first as public intellectuals. Each has contributed to the public good, disrupting, questioning, rethinking. All intentionally made the connection between the university and the public. We see Bill as part of the local board of education; Clif discussing, researching, and writing about public policy; David regularly participating with the public as he writes and contributes to local media and legislative testimony. This work as public intellectual comes with each of them as they become administrators. It informs their actions as administrators and how each of them create spaces for students and academics to engage as public intellectuals—supporting the creation of collectives to act in the local community, building new ways to engage in higher education so the intention is for graduates to be contributing citizens in various contexts, and allocating resources to further sustain advocacy and activism beyond the university walls.

Ways to begin viewing administrators as public intellectuals

In Chaps. 3 and 4, we discuss the different ways to begin to view students and academics as public intellectuals and share related description and in some cases, literature that relates to the work. What we found when considering administrators as public intellectuals is that at times, the administrator acts as a public intellectual but in most moments, it is actually about the administrator creating spaces—often through policy and structure–for students and academics to act. Therefore, the following section reflects this framework.

> 1. *Create spaces for students to engage as public intellectuals*
>
> **Relevant policies and structures: articulation agreements, transfer policies including granting credits, policies related to generating course outcomes and class/unit structures, facilities policies, student code of conduct policies**

Questions to consider:

1. In what ways does the university create pathways for non-traditional students to have access to completing programs of study? How can access to higher education play an important role in supporting students to engage as public intellectuals?

2. How are classes and program plans across discipline structured to support community engagement? In what ways do classes and programs operate from the image of the student as a public intellectual?
3. How often is working towards the public good listed as an outcome to a class, course/program or degree?
4. In what ways is student research positioned with the intention of social change and equity?
5. In what ways does the university create public forums and gatherings for students to lead and engage with local and global issues, acting as public intellectuals?
6. Are there gathering spaces across the university that restrict students in coming together to discuss and debate public issues? In what ways are physical spaces constructed and governed so students can think and act as public intellectuals?

Possible actions:

1. Create articulated pathways across systems and within communities for non-traditional students to easily access higher education.
2. Offer alternative credits towards a degree based in students' life experiences, in particular, community engagement and actions as public intellectuals.
3. Implement policy and structures regarding class/unit outcomes, assignments, and assessments for students to focus on being public intellectuals including engaging in community engagement, social change, equity, and the public good. Create related assessment policies that support longer timelines and ability to respond to assignments in non-traditional manners.
4. Rethink the overall semester schedule and how units/classes are structured to focus on questions and public issues, supporting students to connect theory and practice for relevant solutions. Make visible these ideas to the public for debate and dialogue through forums, publications in local newspapers, and appearances in local media.
5. Offer financial support to students acting as public intellectuals to present research and actions beyond the local community at relevant conferences and meetings.
6. Review and discuss the work of the Local to Global Forum and Festival (see Chap. 6) and take inspiration from this successful program to create a similar forum and festival related to issues in your context. Engage students as public intellectuals to lead and plan the forum and festival with support of administration.
7. Review facility policies and student codes of conduct to support the student as public intellectual, ensuring large gatherings and free speech events are supported. Rethink and rewrite any policies that restrict gatherings of students to engage in discussion and debate (e.g. "free speech zones").

2. Create spaces for academics to engage as public intellectuals

Relevant Policies and Structures: Budgeting, Promotion/Tenure Policies and Structures, Hiring Policies, Funding for Research, Research Structures

Questions to consider:

1. Are there financial resources allocated by administration to support academics as public intellectuals engaging with the local and global community?
2. How are promotion and/or tenure policies and structures supportive of the academic as public intellectual? Does this include impact and engagement with the local and global community?
3. How is research focused on working towards the public good supported through time and other resources by administrations? How are policies and structures governing research, grant writing, and tender application based on the view of the academic as public intellectual? How does administration support research services to further academics' work as public intellectuals?
4. How are academics supported to include students (associate, undergraduate, postgraduate) in research the impacts and engages with local and global communities?
5. In what ways are academics encouraged and supported to include content and activities in teaching that situates both student and academic as public intellectuals, focused on local and global issues? How are assessments and assignments related to this view and focus?
6. How are partnerships with community-based organisations fostered and developed by academics? What administrative supports are necessary to ensure reciprocal relationships?
7. How are academics supported in building pathways for community members to complete degrees and work in community-centered cohorts?
8. Does the academic community at the university include local Indigenous elders and other important community members that do not necessarily fit the traditional academic requirements of a doctoral degree? How is knowledge gathered from the local place recognized as critical to what is studied at the university?
9. Is there a willingness on the part of the administration to incorporate policy direction that emanates from community-based public intellectual engagement?

Possible actions:

1. Rethink budgets and include a priority to support the academic as public intellectual, in particular, engagement with the public.
2. Review promotion/tenure policies with academics to see how academics engage as public intellectuals, specifically, how impact and engagement is articulated and recognised. Create a team of academics and administrators to rethink and

rewrite/write policies focused on supporting and recognising engagement with the public and working towards the public good.
3. Set aside resources directed at an internal grant program to support and encourage academic and student research focused on the public good.
4. Look at how partnership offices at the university are structured and function to see if reciprocal relationships between the university and community-based organisations are commonplace. If this is not evident, then rethink and rewrite policies and structures and offer resources (time, financial) to establish reciprocal partnership building as a priority.
5. Design a robust professor of practice model. This should not an academic, but a community expert who has done the work of fostering the public good (e.g. an activist, or non-profit leader (even a politician or educator) and is willing to work with all levels of academics to create a collaborative model of working as public intellectuals.

3. *Create spaces for administrators to engage as public intellectuals*

Relevant Policies and Structures: Key Performance Indicators (KPI), University Mission Statement, University Goals/Outcomes, Policies Related to Operations, Hiring Practices, Governance Policies, Procedural Policies

Questions to consider:

1. What does it mean to be an administrator engaging as a public intellectual? Does it relate to being an ethical leader? How might administrators define their position as an public intellectual? Does this change depending on the context and the mission of the university? Are ethical and political perspectives part of being an administrator engaging as public intellectual? If so, how?
2. In what ways might an administrator challenge managerialism? In what ways could policy and structures be rethought to create a culture of collaborative process that responds to the university population, supports students and academics as public intellectuals, and moves towards the public good?
3. What might it mean for administration to work from the goal of repositioning higher education as part of the public sphere? What policies and structures would need to change if the university was the public sphere?
4. How often as an administrator is there opportunity to intellectually engage with issues regarding the university population and local community? In what ways is there conversation and debate around the related values? How are these issues incorporated into policies and structures reflecting a full understanding of the realities?
5. How can the commitment of expanding the pool of talent at the university be defined by an administrator? How can this definition be related to acting as a public intellectual as well as making spaces for students and academics to act as

Disrupting the Absurd: Rethinking Structures and Policies ...

public intellectuals? Does this mean rethinking policies, structures, and expected practices (often deemed unofficial policy) to provide opportunities to students, academics, and community-members that might not have been considered for opportunities previously?

6. Does the current organisation of the university support a commitment to anything beyond efficiency and profit-driven decision-making? If not, how can this be disrupted? Rethought? Does it relate to policy and structures? Or is it just a mindset? Can a new mindset work within narrow policies and structures?
7. How often does the administrator follow the academic? What does this look like? Does it change if the administrator views the academic as public intellectual? Does it work if the academic is still viewed as service provider?
8. How often does the administrator follow the student? What does this look like? Does it change if the student is viewed by administrator as a public intellectual? Does it work if the student is still viewed as a customer?

Possible actions:

1. Review the administrative position description and see in what ways the position is situated to support work as a public intellectual. If there is not a direct statement supporting this work, what are the expectations that could be interpreted to support work as a public intellectual? Revise the position description if necessary.
2. Create professional development and activities to support administrators at all levels across the university context to engage as public intellectuals as well as create spaces for academics and students to engage as public intellectuals. This can be imagined in multiple ways. For example, having an online unit or reading group for administrators to participate in that includes a project focused on action as a public intellectual.
3. Review the university or specific college (depending on your administrative role) mission statement and see what commitments the university is making based on this statement. Using these stated commitments, trace how these ideas are being implemented beyond the mission statement. Make these implementations public to the university community. Support a way to make these implementation public to communities beyond the university. This could be through a public forum, media releases, displays in public spaces (government offices, shopping malls, libraries).
4. Support administrators across the university to move beyond the understanding of providing a service and seeing academics as service providers and students as customers to seeing administrators, academics, and students as public intellectuals. Collaboratively look at policy and procedures that are impacted by a "service-minded" perspective and revise these policies and procedures so decision-making is based on the image of the administrator, academic, and student as public intellectual.

References

Bahls, S. (2014). *Shared governance in times of change: A practical guide for universities and colleges*. Washington, DC: AGB Press.

Doran, C. (2016). Managerialism: An ideology and its evolution. *International Journal of Management, Knowledge and Learning, 5*(1), 81–97.

Enteman, W. (1993). *Managerialism: The emergence of a new ideology*. Wisconsin: University of Wisconsin Press.

Fraser, H., & Taylor, N. (2016). *Neoliberalization, universities and the public intellectual*. New York: Palgrave.

Greene, M. (1995). *Releasing the imagination: Essays on education, the arts, and social change*. San Francisco: Jossey-Bass.

Lorenz, C. (2012). If you're so smart, why are you under surveillance? Universities, neoliberalism, and new public management. *Critical Inquiry, 8*(3), 599–629.

Orr, Y., & Orr, R. (2016). The death of Socrates: Managerialism, metrics, and bureaucratisation in universities. *Australian Universities Review, 58*(2), 15–25.

Peters, M., Liu, T., & Ondercin, D. (2012). *The pedagogy of the open society: Knowledge and the governance of higher education*. New York: Springer.

Quiggins, J. (2003). Word for Wednesday. Retrieved from http://johnquiggin.com/2003/07/02/word-for-wednesday-managerialism-definition.

Santiago, R., & Carvalho, T. (2004). Effects of managerialism on the perceptions of higher education in Portugal. *Higher Education Policy, 17*, 427–444.

Santiago, R., & Carvalho, T. (2012). Managerialism rhetorics in Portuguese higher education. *Minerva, 50*, 511–532.

Unpublished manuscript. (2017). *Self-Evaluation Report*. Bellingham, WA: Self-Design Institute.

Unpublished manuscript. (2018). *SDGI Learner Handbook*. Bellingham, WA: Self-Design Institute.

Unpublished manuscript. (2018). *Learner Handbook and Catalog*. Bellingham, WA: Self-Design Institute.

West, D. (2015). The systemic pathologies of university 'managerialism'. *The Sydney Morning Herald*. Retrieved from http://www.smh.com.au/comment/the-systemic-pathologies-of-university-managerialism-20151030-gkmoti.html.

Chapter 6
The Practice of Hope Across the University

> *After all, we are not so violently bent upon our own opinions as to reject any offer proposed by wise men, which shall be found equally innocent, cheap, easy, and effectual. But before something of that kind shall be advanced in contradiction to our scheme, and offering a better, we desire the author or authors will be pleased maturely to consider two points. First, as things now stand, how they will be able to create an organization that perpetuates neoliberalism on such a large scale. And secondly, how will they change millions of these students in human figure throughout these institutions, who believe their sole purpose is to becomes critical thinkers and graduate as citizens willing to question, willing to disrupt, and willing to think beyond neoliberalism, adding more thinkers to the bulk of already existing population that see themselves as public intellectuals and activists for change.*
>
> **The absurd:** *...First, as things now stand, how they will be able to create an organization that perpetuates neoliberalism on such a large scale. And secondly, how will they change millions of these students in human figure throughout these institutions, who believe their sole purpose is to becomes critical thinkers and graduate as citizens willing to question, willing to disrupt, and willing to think beyond neoliberalism...*

The practice of hope, and in particular students, academics, and administrators acting as public intellectuals has relevance beyond schools of education. How do we move our ideas to a large scale? How do we engage the many students across the university? As we continued to talk about our work with colleagues, people said to us, you need to talk to this person or you need to see what they are doing in this place. We were intrigued, moving beyond schools of education seemed to be the next step in this work. So more conversations over food happened, gathering together in university cafes and restaurants adjacent to large research conferences. Emails exchanged furthering articulation of ideas, questions, and implementations. More

© Springer Nature Singapore Pte Ltd. 2019
J. M. Iorio and C. S. Tanabe, *Higher Education and the Practice of Hope*,
Rethinking Higher Education, https://doi.org/10.1007/978-981-13-8645-9_6

stories emerged, stories that illustrate how disciplines outside of education create structures and policies that disrupt neoliberalism in higher education. These examples demonstrate practices of hope.

Description 1: School of Social Transformation

School of Social Transformation

At Arizona State University, the School of Social Transformation (SST) located in the College of Liberal Arts and Sciences offers a strong example of multidisciplinary work "to create social change that is democratic, inclusive, and just" (https://sst.clas.asu.edu/). This school brings together faculty across five interdisciplinary fields to create an unique program focused on justice, engaging with diversity, and understanding how social, historical, and cultural aspects create society. Thinking with the local and global communities, equality is central to acting as an advocate and activist employing actions to change the world.

Programs in School of Social Transformation include African and African American Studies, Asian and Pacific American Studies, Women and Gender Studies, Justice and Social Inquiry, and Social and Cultural Pedagogy. Undergraduate and graduate majors, minors, and certificates support multiple entry and exits points into the coursework. With opportunities for researching with faculty and over 180 internships available across the United States, students are supported to connect with the public as well as develop relationships with both faculty and professionals in the field. Spaces are created for students to question and rethink through supportive relationships with faculty and professionals, discovering "how to create change that is democratic, inclusive, and just" (https://sst.clas.asu.edu/node/478). Students graduate with the ability to work in advocacy organisations, law firms, education settings, domestic violence shelters, intelligence organisations, social work, government work, museums, refugee resettlement organisations, and universities.

Beyond coursework, the School of Social Transformation offers ways to engage in the tenets of the program. For example, the Simon Ortiz and Labriola Center Lecture on Indigenous Land, Culture, and Community lecture series highlights the Indigenous American views and experiences seeking "to create and celebrate knowledge that evolves from an inclusive Indigenous worldview and that is applicable to all walks of life" (https://english.clas.asu.edu/indigenous#about). Speakers in this series are representative of a variety of disciplines including politics, humanities, arts, and sciences and discuss a range of subjects. All the lectures are free and open to the public. Speakers include poet, novelist, essayist, and environmentalist Linda Hogan (Chickasaw) sharing her work through narrative, Arlinda Locklear (Lumbee), the first American Indian woman to argue a case before the United States Supreme Court lecturing on tribal land claims and federal Indian law, and Kathryn Shanty (Assiniboine), an academic mapping Native American voice in higher education.

Description 1: School of Social Transformation 105

Through the John P. Frank Memorial Lecture (part of an endowed series), speakers focus on critical and current issues of justice. This series has featured United States Supreme Court Associate Justices Sonia Sotomayor, Ruth Bader Ginsburg, and Sandra Day O'Connor, legal scholar Anita Hill, and former Labor Secretary, Robert Reich. These and other SST events are offered free to campus and community.

Humanities Behind the Walls is a project lead by Alan E. Gomez and H.L.T. Quan, both Associate Professors in the School of Social Transformation. This project draws on a genealogy of situated and subjugated knowledges that have emerged from behind prison walls to provide an opportunity for faculty and students to critically engage the humanistic and humanizing potential inherent in acts of reading and discussing literature, poetry, and drama with people incarcerated at Perryville Women's Prison, and with formerly incarcerated people at Arizona State University (https://ihr.asu.edu/research/seed/humanities-behind-walls-hbw). Components of this project include reading circles inside Perryville Prison and at ASU with formerly incarcerated people (both led by ASU faculty and graduate students), seminars and workshops led by interdisciplinary scholars, families, and formerly incarcerated people, and bringing together a collective of scholars supporting the work to further develop the work beyond ASU.

Centers that are part of the School of Social Transformation consider current issues of justice and equity. For example, the Center for Gender Equity in Science and Technology, which was an extension of the COMPUGIRLS project (under the direction of Professor Kimberly Scott) focuses on bringing together policymakers, practitioners, and scholars to engage with research and create ways to "break down the systemic barriers that prevent girls and women of color—African American, Native American, Latina or Asian American, for example—from studying in STEM fields and pursuing related careers" (https://asunow.asu.edu/content/asu-launches-new-center-empower-women-color-stem). With a commitment to advocacy, capacity building, and knowledge, the Center implements projects that reflect these responsibilities. For instance, COMPUGIRLS furthers the capacity building facet of the center by increasing STEM participation of women and girls of color through a technology program that "weds culturally relevant practices with project-based technology activities encouraging girls of color to develop socially relevant, researched products in areas of digital media, coding, and robotics" (https://cgest.asu.edu/capacity).

Another center located within the School of Social Transformation is the Center for Indian Education, directed by Professor Bryan Brayboy. In existence for over 50 years and publishing the *Journal of American Indian Education*, this center's mission is constantly being reviewed and rethought to respond to the current context and needs, emphasizing a deep-rooted responsibility to Indigenous nations of Arizona and to Arizona State University. Further, the center is committed to research and the support of "a new generation of Indigenous scholars, and our involvement with a global community of scholars, policy makers, and practitioners in Indigenous education" https://center-for-indian-education.asu.edu/our-vision). Several projects are part of the center, including the Gila River Early Educators Attaining Teaching Excellence (GRE2ATE). This project funded by a Professional Development Grant from the U.S. Department of Education/Office of Indian Education enrolled 16

Native American participants in the Arizona State University interdisciplinary bachelor degree program with a concentration in early childhood and is delivered within the Gila River Indian Community.

> Mario Molina, Tribal Education director for the Gila River Indian Community, sees the program as a sustainable model for instruction that will build capacity from within the community. "The GRE^{2}ATE program will provide my community an opportunity to develop our own teaching cadre that will recognize and encompass the essence of the Akimel O'Otham and Pee Posh culture, language and heritage as we teach our young members," says Molina. "We see this as a positive attribute that will help sustain the community for years and generations to come, and will serve as a model of instruction that we hope will work in concert with the beliefs that we hold dear as an indigenous community."
>
> https://center-for-indian-education.asu.edu/content/asu-gila-river-partner-preparing-early-childhood-educators

Another project administered by the Center is the Gila River Culture and Language Teacher Cohort (GRCLTC), an accelerated 4 + 1 program where students received a BA/MA in Interdisciplinary Studies with a concentration in Indigenous Education. GRCLTC is supported through a grant with the Gila River Indian Community (GRIC) Tribal Education Department. The purpose of this program is to prepare culture and language teachers to work in schools in the Gila River Indian Community. Eight students completed their BA and five students completed their MA. All students have a strong commitment to their Tribal community for the preservation and revitalization of their Akimel O'Otham language and to ensure that young children and families are taught their culture and language. Like the GRE^{2}ATE project, all academic courses were held within the Gila River Indian Community.

Further, two Pueblo Ph.D. cohorts, totalling 16, have also graduated from ASU in a collaborative project with the Santa Fe (New Mexico) Indian School Leadership Institute, providing leadership and research capacity for several of the 19 Pueblos. All coursework was facilitated close to the participants' pueblos and all alumni are continuing to provide leadership in their communities. This collaborative program was funded by the Kellogg Foundation and has been nationally recognized.

The center also hosts The *Journal of American Indian Education*, started in 1961, and features scholarship discussing education issues of American Indians, Alaska Natives, Native Hawaiians, and Indigenous peoples worldwide, including First Nations, Māori, Aboriginal/Torres Strait Islander peoples, and Indigenous peoples of Latin America, Africa, and others (https://jaie.asu.edu/). An online Masters degree in Indigenous Education is being launched in January, 2019.

The School of Social Transformation creates multiple opportunities for students, academics, and administrators to engage as public intellectuals. The structure of the multidisciplinary programs, access to research and experiences, and variety of current issues and relevant contexts reflect an intent of thinking, questioning, disrupting, and rethinking, rather than profit and cost-effectiveness. The program is about action as hope, engagement as hope, and it offers places for people to enact change.

A Story: Acting as Public Intellectual Within and Beyond the School of Social Transformation

We meet at a busy cafe in a city—in the shadow of the large convention center hosting an international research conference. The establishment hums with many people, books, and servers moving in and out of the square tables, couches, and tall stools throughout the space. We find ourselves sitting towards the back wall—Jeanne has known Beth Blue Swadener, a well-established scholar and professor, for several years. This is the first time she is meeting Clif. Clif moves through his introduction and the two make some connections across their education and careers. The conversation moves to our intent as we have identified colleagues, people we have known through other work, collaborations, and related fields that we see as public intellectuals practicing hope. Beth's work is not only known by us but across the field of education and social justice. The personal stories she shares with us throughout our conversation illustrate her strong relationships with her undergraduate and graduate students based on framing arguments and working towards critical change—this scholar is committed to equity and humanity.

One read of her personal essay on the university website tells you her values, beliefs, and actions—and how these are part of her daily work,

> Having benefited from excellent mentoring from my professors at the University of Wisconsin-Madison, I have tried throughout my career to pay it forward in a number of ways–with over 100 doctoral mentees in three universities in the U.S. and two abroad (in Kenya and Greece). This essay is a brief reflection on the ways in which an "ally" approach, anchored in social justice, permeates my work as a mentor. All of my degrees have reflected interdisciplinary study and I have long crossed academic borders and mentored students in several fields. Principles of social justice and inclusion have informed my research and collaborative work with students in the fields of childhood studies, early childhood and special education, policy studies, and, most recently, justice studies. My mentorship is organic, participatory and grounded in my work in unlearning oppression and alliance building across difference. It is also grounded in the belief that all doctoral students have an array of funds of knowledge, can complete a strong dissertation and will disseminate their scholarship and impact the field.

(https://graduate.asu.edu/odm/elizabeth-beth-blue-swadener)

Beth understands a public intellectual as a person recognizing privilege, and, in some cases, 'claiming the margins' as she cites bell hooks. Writing letters to the editor, communicating with elected officials, engaging in anti-colonial and exploring convivial research—all actions in academics engaging as public intellectuals. Her own program of work includes herself as an activist scholar, "doing" events, raising awareness, mobilizing, networking—building coalitions and alliances so people can stand with each other. Providing a space where people can talk to each other—especially people that might not talk to each other is critical. And this comes alive in the annual Local to Global Justice Forum and Festival, in its 15th year at the time of our discussion. This is where community activists, students and faculty come together to connect local issues in Arizona to global struggles. Nothing about us without us–a mantra she shares as describes the forum and festival and ways it seeks *to flatten hierarchies in a teach-in and festival environment. Each year the student, faculty and community planning team raises between $10 and 12,000 (primarily from University organizations and schools) to keep this event free and open to all. The work is bolstered by students from many majors and seasoned community activists meeting for months and using social media and communication via other events to get out the word each year.*

Local to Global Justice Organization and Annual Gathering

> Local to Global Justice was founded in 2001 by students in Education, Justice Studies and Law at ASU-Tempe. The group is currently composed of students, faculty, and community members and is open to everyone.
>
> Our primary goal is to educate ASU students and the greater community about issues of local and global justice, while promoting diversity, freedom of speech, and academic freedom of discussion. We believe it is vital to connect local diversity, sustainability, and social justice issues to larger global struggles.
>
> (http://www.localtoglobal.org/plan.html)

Started by faculty and graduate students in 2001, Local to Global Justice (LTGJ) is a group of activist-scholars identifying the power of organizing and acting in the community. Beth Blue Swadener, an advisor to the group since its inception, recognizes that "the organization has always been about having a space for local and regional activists to gather, exchange information and connect "local issues to global struggles", highlighting a variety of issues rather than just one, "We're the opposite of a single-issue group," she said. "We are a big umbrella or a large tent" (Buechler, 2017). School of Social Transformation graduate student Jeremy Omori and program coordinator for L2GJ shares the intent of the organization—"to bring together community members, students, as well as faculty members to come together and talk about issues and best practices for social justices... ...In my opinion, it's a wonderful way to get involved in all levels of activism, especially for those who might be intimidated by the whole idea of activism, but they want to do something" (Buechler, 2017).

The largest event the group plans each year is the Local to Global Justice Festival and Forum. Formerly know as the "Teach-in" (inspired by the "teach-ins" of the 1960s, where people convened to learn about political and social issues), this forum and festival is about everyone contributing in sharing knowledge. Focussing first on issues of corporate globalization and then, in response to 9/11 and the Patriot Act, addressing civil liberties, this annual event recognizes "that everyone has something to teach and something to learn" (http://www.localtoglobal.org/festival.html). Included in the program are "hands-on exhibits and workshops, as well as activities and workshops for children and youth, and tabling from over 40 community groups" as well as music, local artists, performances, and food. And everything is free of charge. Sponsors for the forum and festival include schools and committees across ASU and local community businesses and groups.

Previous festival and forums have addressed issues including justice for women, solidarity through knowledge and action, dialogues for healing and renewal, food justice, and re-storying community. In 2016, the theme of racial justice focused on "strengthening alliances against racism and other forms of oppression" as

> Conversations and contestations over racial justice have fueled nation-wide debates over police brutality, housing quality and gentrification, poverty, economic and educational disparity, access to food, transportation and health care. In the order to recognize racial justice as a driving, divisive, but also potentially unifying theme, we will bring together local, national, and international educators, activists, and community members to learn and engage in dialogue about issues relating to racial justice.
>
> (program, 2016)

Sessions on reproductive rights and racial justice, microaggressions and their implications in youth of color, activism, building coalitions, Islamic nonviolence, civic engagement, sexism, roots of racism, and peace building are just some of the topics. Workshops, yoga, art-making, music, discussions, and food work in conjunction with the sessions offer multiple entry points into the issue.

One forum held February 24–26, 2017 lead with the theme Community Justice: Alliances for Actions. Speakers, workshop leaders, and artists came together to consider ways of actions towards justice and equity,

> The 2017 event theme, ***Community Justice: Alliances for Action***, recognizes that social movements gain momentum when visionaries, community leaders, activists, and those committed to social justice have a chance to form alliances across communities, cities, states, and nations. Arizona has a rich history of activist alliances, including the César Chávez movement in the 1960 and 1970s, the on-going struggle to re-establish Ethnic Studies programs, the fight to protect Indigenous land and water, and the ongoing fight against racial profiling and discrimination infused by state legislation SB1070 and recent executive orders that threaten mass deportations and human rights. The same principles apply anywhere in the world where justice is at stake: no single individual, organization, or policy can bring about change. "Justice" is inseparable from "community."
>
> (http://www.localtoglobal.org/2017.html)

In 2018, the theme for the forum and festival was "Compassionate Resistance" reflecting on the current administration in the United States and large global concerns with the hope to "inform future actions and resistance movements, both locally and abroad. The forum specifically focusing on" standing "in solidarity, community building, and face-to-face interactions, to continue building momentum for progressive changes inspired by hope, care, and compassion for each other and our communities" (https://localtoglobal.org/2018.html). Inclusive to the forum and festival was a community action day, panels discussing resistance and immigration, art performances and activities, as well as yoga and mediation practices.

The act of creating a space and time through this festival and forum to learn, develop, and engage practices of activism is two-fold. First, it offers an opportunity for practice and action within the frame of the university context and, at the same time, support practice and action in the public—locally and globally. In a recent study (Farago, Swadener, Richter, Eversman, & Roca-Servat, 2018), findings indicate the forum and festival "benefited students academically, professionally, and personally in intersecting and intertwining ways" (p. 154). This included how activism supported "scholar-activism, critical thinking, applied learning, career and professional development, leadership development, and community engagement and activism" (p. 154). Further, the research indicated how the forum and festival became a way for communities and the university to connect. What is documented through the research is the principles of LTGJ and how those principles are critical to creating "socially transformative places"—

- Partnering with communities,
- Centering social justice,
- Developing critical consciousness,
- Foregrounding egalitarian structures and relationships,
- Connecting to broad social movements.

(p. 168)

Thinking with Social Justice—Coursework and Action Coming Together

The School of Social Transformation works to contest neoliberalism in both higher education and within local and global communities. Coursework and engagement in social issues (for example, through the Local to Global Festival and Forum and the Human Rights Film Festival) empowers students with the foundational knowledge and discourse to debate, challenge, resist, and rethink within the context of the university and then in the public. This becomes evident as alumni from this program illustrate these actions. For example, Dr. Matthew Desmond now a sociologist at Harvard University, recipient of the MacArthur Genius Grant, and author of *Evicted: Poverty and Profit in the American City* (2016) is a graduate of the Justice Studies program at ASU. He cites his experience at ASU in his coursework and ability to engage in student activism and community service as integral in shaping his work towards equity. Another illustration of the impact of this program is graduate Dr. Luis Fernandez. Dr. Hernandez is the currently a Professor at Northern Arizona University and leads the Society for the Study of Social Programs. He is co-founder of the Local to Global Justice group as well as Repeal Coalition, a grassroots immigration rights group. His writing discusses social movements and includes the text *Policing Dissent: Social Contract and the Anti-globalization Movement* (2008).

Higher education has the ability to disrupt the limitations of neoliberalism and when an institute is constructed to do just that, democracy and social equity become a possibility. The work of Beth Blue Swadener, Local to Global Justice, and alumni of the School of Social Transformation epitomize a commitment of what it means to be ethical and political in higher education and in the public. The spaces created by the structures and policies in the School of Social Transformation are the supports needed to empower the people of an institution to engage and mentor students, colleagues, and the public towards change.

Description 2: Bachelor of Arts

The disruption of accepted higher education practices and resistance of standardization across university coursework in conjunction with the purpose of a program situated in social change and equity, engaging as a public intellectual can be realised. A strong example of this is a Bachelors of Arts program serving students representative of low socioeconomic status, first-in-family to attend university, lower entry levels, Indigenous, full-time working, full-time domestic responsibilities, rural and remote communities, and immigrant and refugee populations. This non-traditional cohort offers the possibilities of creating higher education structures that support the engagement and empowerment of these students to complete a degree in higher education.

With awareness of how the higher education sector is driven by profit-making and related decision-making, academics creating this program choose to privilege the ethical and pedagogical first. This meant understanding who the university and this program would serve and how this would influence the structures of the program. For example, in noting the population of the program would include first-in-family, this construct was unpacked by the academics and a shared meaning was created:

> It is worth reminding ourselves of what the idea of 'first in family' really means for both the student and the teacher and our assessment practices ...
>
> 1. Students do not have family to seek advice from about what to do and how to get on at University. University culture appears as a mystery and decoding mechanisms are not readily available. This is one of the reasons students make the very big mistake of reverting to 'school knowledge'.
> 2. Students are less likely to have exposure to the kinds of codes and language structures that shape university culture. That is, the elaborate and formal language of academic discourse appears as gobbledygook (Bernstein, 1964).
>
> (Ashton, 2015)

This deep and shared understanding of the population contributes to how structures are created within the program. Structures include supportive pedagogy founded in the diversity of the group and desire to create discursive spaces (Carr, 2014) in collaboration with integrated curriculum. Utilizing Discourse-Based Assessment Practices (Moraitis, Carr, & Daddow, 2012) as a source of empowerment for students to build the cultural capital to success in higher education as well as strategies to define the identity of the student and a sense of belonging within the university community are aligned with the population. This comprehension of creating structures reflective of the non-traditional student disrupts the historical and social construct of the higher education reflecting the actions of the academics as public intellectual but also creating the space and support needed for students to engage as public intellectuals. Paul Ashton, the previous coordinator of the course shares,

> One of the key things I think about our approach is that we/I am deeply committed to the idea that all students should have access to the ideas that are usually partitioned for the middle class. Complex and difficult ideas can be taught to all if the context for such

learning is created. We never shirk on the ideas, we just make it really explicit (where to draw lines is obviously a real challenge. For me, the student needs to see themselves as part of the conversation. However, this position in the discussion is not a liberal birthright, rather it is an achieved position. One has the right to speak because they engage in (and produce) public discourse. There may not be many hard and fast truths in the world, but what truth/understanding we do have is produced in the debate itself (even something like the law of gravity is a product of scientific debate even if it is concretely true). Is it more true than saying that justice requires equality? For example, the question of what an education is answered in the debate about education. Of course, we get the answers we deserve, if our debate is impoverished so will the answers be. Learning is thus an ethical act.

(Personal email, 2017)

Ashton (2015) refers the structures governing the program as "rhizomic organisation" as all parts of the program are interconnected. Academics work in integrated teams where responsibility is shared in terms of the entire program, rather than the usual academic allocation of the individual class with little or no connection across the overall program. Considerations of the group include content associations crossing classes and thinking with the students as they move through each class. "Students are considered as members of a course of study rather than as enrollments in individual (seemingly unrelated) units" (Ashton, 2015). The technical of the timetabling and delivery of the classes is addressed through "unified delivery" including an "organisational cluster" of approximately 100 students. This cluster is lead by one academic creating a space for dynamic and collaborative relationships between student and academic. The relationship aspect of this program is critical to creating empowered spaces for students. As the academic and student develop the relationship, students are also placed into fixed social groups. These groups remain consistent and become a powerful space of debate, discussion, and support. Ashton adds,

What we found was that when we could get the groups relating outside of class this really helped all aspects of the approach. We have/had these great parties at the Dancing Dog (a local pub) where students would perform a song, read some poetry or cut some moves on the dance floor and they created some good friendships and a real sense that we were doing something simply by putting themselves out there and taking a risk in front of new friends. Of course, this would involve us teachers leading the way by humiliating ourselves on stage first through a poetry reading or some such thing.

(Personal email, 2017)

The academics involved in this program are not only strong educators but scholars in the field and committed members of the university. Their engagement includes creative outputs, publications, editing journals and texts, and active members of advisory and academics boards/committees. Further, these academics demonstrate an implied understanding of how teaching is a political and ethical practice in their awareness of the responsibilities of working with non-traditional students. This includes the ability to work multidisciplinary inclusive of deconstruction and understanding the discourse within higher education. All of these components contribute to how they construct themselves as teacher and illustrate the academic as public intellectual.

An example of how this looks in the classroom is the student assignment creating an argumentative essay. This essay is structured to develop students academic language. The essay uses activities framed by the work of McCormack (2002) focused on teaching students to read and write academic discourse, and then refined through in-class debate, utilizing fours moves as fundamental facets "of the essay as a form, of learning and engaging with ideas, and of being a speaker" (Personal, email, 2017) and include:

1. fairly and generously demonstrate knowledge of the other position;
2. critique this position;
3. outline your superior position; and
4. make a concession to the other position or acknowledge that your position is not perfect.

Most of the unit (two/thirds) is dedicated to exploring possible ideas to structure the essay around. While the unit is delivered, the structure of debate is aligned with the structure of essay—essentially, the content of the class models the essay. This positions the necessity of the student to use academic language to complete the essay assignment. Explicit teaching on how to write the essay is part of the class work and includes one-on-one interactions and consultations with an academic. This structure is an example of how students are re-positioned as public intellectuals, empowered to question assumptions, disrupts accepted ways of knowing, and resist the student as consumer expectation.

Description 3: A Proposal to Working Across Disciplines

Three people come together in the crowded university cafe—two academics from education, one academic from the arts. The conversation begins as they share the frustrations of the new organization of the merger, colleges of arts and education becoming one. The moving of offices and campuses, creating chaos. But in the chaos there is hope as a small collective of academics attempting to practice hope come together to create something new. The conversation now moves to collaboration. In what ways might we better empower students to engage as public intellectuals? And what spaces might we create to support practices as public intellectuals? Can cross-disciplinary commitments challenge the neoliberal culture of this university towards rethinking beyond the bottom-line?

Cost-effective strategies like closing down campuses and combining colleges has offered programs unique opportunities in responding to these neoliberal decisions. With the merger of two colleges, the bringing together of degree programs to one campus offers an opportunity to combine classes to create unique multidisciplinary degrees. For example, arts and education proposed an unique undergraduate program with the prime purpose of creating spaces for students to engage as public intellectuals.

The first year of the program would be situated in the arts with classes on reason, philosophy, media, thought, and activism/advocacy. While the foundation of the classes is arts, each class is being rethought as a collaborative space where early childhood academics are teaming with arts academics to bring together disciplines.

The intent of this year is to build the students' understanding of how to think, how to build theory, and develop an understanding of the ethical, political, social, and historical aspects of society. All of this contributes to developing democratic citizens of local and global communities willing to ask questions, disrupt assumptions and oppressive doctrines, and act to change. Specifically, these classes emphasize how teaching does not happen in a vacuum but rather is always political. This tenet changes how educators become and a new lens on technical of being a teacher is offered.

The second year would entail students developing a minor in arts while beginning education units. The minor builds the identity of the teacher beyond just the technical methods as students are invited to explore deeply a specific art. This year is also the first site of working in the community as each semester in the second year involves a class that includes a short placement experience working in a free community-based program monetarily supported by the university. The coming together of the arts, education, and connection to the community provides a concrete experience of engaging as public intellectual. This experience becomes a model for students to draw from and reimagine as they work in the world.

The third and fourth year would focus primarily on classes needed for registration as a teacher but these classes are also inclusive of creating spaces for students to engage as public intellectuals. Advocacy, activism, ethics, and thinking *with* are all part of the coursework. Placing these ideas alongside the methods of teaching continues to provide a lens for understanding the purpose of teaching beyond building children's skills. When students in higher education engage as public intellectuals and become teachers, teachers act in the field as public intellectuals and create spaces for children to act as public intellectuals.

Disrupting the Absurd: Rethinking Structures and Policies to Support Working Across the University

The three examples shared here offer ways to think about how to practice hope across the university. This is evident in the work of the Local to Global forum where all participants are committing to ideas of the public intellectual. They are "wide-awake" and aware of how everyone connected with the forum, including the local public, have something to offer when thinking and acting on local and global issues. In the Bachelor of Arts program, we can see what happens outside college of education when students are first situated as public intellectuals and when academics see this view of student as their responsibility. This becomes even more poignant as this example illustrates what happens in higher education when the population the university serves is part of how the program is conceived and implemented. The School of Social Transformation and proposed undergraduate education/arts program offer both large and small examples of how to think multidisciplinary and what is possible when disciplines and "professional" programs are collaborative. Returning back to the framework of listening, dialogue, and action, we consider the variety of policies and structures that could support implementation of these and similar ideas.

Ways to begin working across the university

1. *Creating spaces and ways to gather*

Relevant Policies and Structures: Governing Space/Facilities Policies, Timetable, Assessment and Teaching

The Local to Global Justice is about education within the university and the community the university serves. With a membership of students, faculty, and community members, this unique group challenges the walls of higher education and finds relevant and impactful ways to situate the university as part of the public. The commitments of this group are rooted in diversity, freedom, and democracy. Further, the creation of multiple spaces for debate and dialogue provide rich examples of the how academics and students can act as public intellectuals. Every year to support the yearly forum, this group and the planning raise over $10,000 to ensure the forum remains free and open to the public. Access to these experiences whether you are part of the university or the surrounding public is clearly important and further demonstrates what it means when a university thinks *with* the community.

Questions to Consider:

1. In what ways does the cultural of a university think and act towards social justice and equity?
2. How are policies and structures conceived and implemented in order to ensure action of the university community in relationship with the issues and needs of the local communities? How does this also translate into the university in relationship with the issues and needs of the global communities? How do budgets and financial?
3. In what ways do academics commit to engaging with the public towards social change and equity? How might academics' commitments create spaces for students to build similar engagements?
4. In what ways do the physical spaces of a campus support small and large gatherings? Are there specific codes and policies that exist to support all kinds of gatherings? If not, what needs to change about these codes and policies to support gatherings that connect the university and the public?

Possible Actions:

1. Begin by holding public forums (inclusive of community members, students, staff, administrators) identifying the local and global community issues. Create lists and priorities of what the university and community collaboration could offer the public in terms of these issues.
2. Commit to events that connect public and university around relevant issues. The context is important here as issues may be different depending on context.
3. Find ways for academics and administrators to support events through fundraising, free use of space, or connections to programs.
4. Make public what is happening at the university in order to involve more community members and university staff and students.
5. Create a culture of debate and dialogue around issues in the university and public. Abandon managerialism practices that create faux participation in the decision-making process for real democratic practices that are messy and reflect real voices and commitments of all stakeholders.
6. Review codes, policies, and procedures that govern how space is used on the campus to ensure all kinds of gatherings are possible. Further, look to see how public and campus spaces can be connected in order to further relationships between the university and the public.

2. *Rethinking and creating programs (regardless of discipline)*

Relevant Policies: Procedures for Creating and Implementing Programs, Timetable, Student and Academic Expectations/Outcomes

The Bachelor of Arts example is a strong way to consider how the student and academic as public intellectual are put into practice outside of colleges of education. In this instance, there are clear practices of collaboration, awareness of student population and academics' strengths, and willingness to imagine and implement a program that is not what is the expected in the profit-driven climate of higher education.

Questions to Consider:

1. In what ways do current programs support the entire population of students in engaging fully with all activities within the program?
2. What policies and practices need to be revised in order to support students in thinking with the content of a class and/or program in regard to the local context and population of the university?
3. In what ways do current programs indicate awareness of local and global context? Do programs run as if they are contextless?
4. What actions in preparation, teaching, and assessments do academics practice in order to ensure concrete support of student population?

5. Is collaboration with colleagues part of the culture of a program and/or institution? How do you know? What policies, structures, and practices exist to support collaboration?

Possible Actions:

1. Determine who the students are that a program is serving. Using this data, build the timetable so it aligns with the needs and requirements of the student population. For example, if most students need to use public transport, use the public transport schedule to create the timetable. Collaborate across disciplines and colleges if necessary.
2. Review teaching policies, structures, and practices to see how content is relevant locally and globally. If policies, structures, and practices are more contextless, rethink in order to have the policies, structures, and practices that engage with local and global issues and communities.
3. Find time and spaces for academics to come together to discuss and rethink in a variety of ways including in-person and virtually. This should be part of the work rather than an extra add-on.

---

3. *Creating multidisciplinary programs*

Relevant Policies and Structures: Course Management Systems, Procedures for Creating and Implements New Programs, Publication and Presentation Policies Related to Tenure and Promotion

While multidisciplinary programs are innovative, at times, structures and policies exist that may impede the implementation. For example, codes for programs can fall into separate categories, not allowing for combination into one degree. Therefore, structure and policy can stop implementation of the multidisciplinary program. This presents a mismatch between the conceptual, pedagogical, and technical. In this sense, the technical is the structures and policies—while the pedagogical and conceptual are situated in the multidisciplinary collaboration. How does this response provoke thinking towards something beyond the separation of discipline and classifications governing program creation and implementation?

On the other hand, the School of Social Transformation has taken the idea of multidisciplinary and created programs that respond to relevant issues and contexts, moving beyond the structures dictated by systems and policies. With the intent "to create social change that is democratic, inclusive, and just" (https://sst.clas.asu.edu/), five different disciplines are gathered to create unique programs that impact and engage locally and globally. Specific centres, internships, and lecture series all contribute to the multiple entry points for students to build active relationships with the public. This is evident as the stories of the alumni reflect deep and complex work with communities, engaging and acting in real issues towards social change.

Questions to consider:

1. When collaboration across disciplines creates a new and unique offering for students to engage as public intellectuals, connecting education beyond the university, should this be the impetus to change structures and policies?
2. Should the technical be the primary framework for creating programs in the university setting?
3. What structures and policies are needed to work across disciplines?
4. In what ways do programs commit to equity and social change? How often is this outrightly stated in the program documents? How often are the activities of the program and actions of the students and academics reflective of these commitments?
5. What procedures need to be re-thought in order to support innovative programs?
6. What are the entry points students and academics have to create relationships with local and global communities?

Possible actions:

1. Review and revise structures and policies governing the establishment of multidisciplinary programs to support a multidisciplinary understanding and approach including multiple means into implementation across disciplines.
2. As an university, study the work at length in the School of Social Transformation. Decide what from this program could inspire your own university context.
3. Review program intentions to understand how often social change and equity are the primary goal of a program. If this is not part of current programs at an university, find ways to make this commitment. Beginning with one program is one way to start this process. Work to make a plan of furthering social change and equity across the entire university.
4. Support faculty, staff, students, and administration to collaborate across disciplines including presentation and publications to demonstrate what is possible in higher education.
5. Write new procedures for creating new programs and classes where conceptual and pedagogical frame the technical (class sizes, timetable, assessments). Create related forms and documents that support these practices.

References

Ashton, P. (2015). *Scaffolding learning for success*. Victoria Unversity Leaning and Teaching Symposium: Good Practice and Messy Problems, Victoria University.
Buechler, A. (2017). Local to Global justice advocates for spectrum of social issues at ASU. *State Press*. Retrieved from http://www.statepress.com/article/2017/02/spcampus-spaudio-local-to-global-justice-organization-advocate-for-human-rights-and-environment.
Carr, A. (2014). *Found in translation: Academic knowledge and language learning in discipline-linked transition pedagogies*. Thesis, VUIR, Victoria University.
Desmond, M. (2016). *Evicted: Poverty and profit in the American city*. New York: Crown.

References

Farago, F., Swadener, B. B., Richter, J., Eversman, K., & Roca-Servat, D. (2018). Local to global justice: Roles of student activism in higher education, leadership development, and community engagement. *Alberta Journal of Educational Research, 64*(2), 154–172.

Hernandez, L. (2008). *Policing dissent: Social contract and the anti-globalization movement.* New Jersey: Rutgers University Press.

McCormack, R. (2002). *Learning to learn: The next step: Teaching adults how to read and write the academic discourse.* Melbourne: Language Australia for Victoria University.

Moraitis, P., Carr, A., & Daddow, A. (2012). Developing and sustaining new pedagogies: A case for embedding language, literacy and academic skills in vocational education curriculum. *International Journal of Training Research, 10*(1), 58–72.

Chapter 7
How to Rethink Your University

We desire those politicians who dislike our overture, and may perhaps be so bold to attempt an answer, that they will first ask the students whether they would not at this day think it a great happiness to have become a docile and simple citizen as we prescribe, and thereby have avoided such a perpetual scene of misfortunes as they engage as thinkers and having to oppose and resist in the name of equity and social justice.

We profess, in the sincerity of our hearts, that we have not the least personal interest in endeavoring to promote this necessary work of neoliberalism, having no other motive than the public good, and continuing the pleasure of the rich.

The absurd: *...a great happiness to become a docile and simple citizen as we prescribe, and thereby have avoided such a perpetual scene of misfortunes as they engage as thinkers and having to oppose and resist in the name of equity and social justice.*

After World War II, in a city in the of Reggio Emilia, Italy, a collective of women and the National Liberation Committee (CLN) came together to start a school. This school built out of the bricks of destroyed building from the war and funded by the sale of horse, trunks, and a war tank abandoned by the German army, marked the beginning of a system of early childhood centers representative of political activism, social awareness, and innovation, "arguably, the most successful, most extensive and most sustained example of radical or progressive education that has ever been" (Moss, 2016, p. 167). The community of Reggio Emilia engaged as thinkers, opposing and resisting the histories of fascism in order to create places of participatory democracy.

With infant-toddler centers and preschools for children ages 0–6, this educational and participatory project (as what these schools are known as) understand "that school as first and foremost a public space and site for ethical and political practice—a place of encounter and connection, interaction and dialogue among citizens, young and

© Springer Nature Singapore Pte Ltd. 2019
J. M. Iorio and C. S. Tanabe, *Higher Education and the Practice of Hope*,
Rethinking Higher Education, https://doi.org/10.1007/978-981-13-8645-9_7

older, living together in a community" (Dahlberg & Moss, 2006, p. 2). These schools endeavor to action education as a democratic process in a post-fascist Italy as "long traditions of collective life, cohesive communities, producing norms of reciprocity and trust and networks of civic engagement" (p. 9). Part of this is the consistent image of the child as capable, a foundational value that informs the participation of children as contributing citizens in a democratic community. Further, the participation of parents, families, children, educators, and the local community in these schools is paramount to a process of meaning-making; meaning-making that creates "new sites for democratic politics while at the same time, extending the scope of politics to new areas."

(p. 12)

Pedagogies focused on making listening, thinking, and learning visible create a space where multiple intentions, contestations, and interpretations are welcomed and expected, illustrating school as a place of democracy. Policy and structures exist to support these practices. Policy like The Nido Law (passed in 1972) supporting women to participate fully in the postwar society by offering funding and construction of nidi (nests) for children ages 3 months through 3 years–essentially establishing the care and education of young children as the responsibility of the public. Evolution of the law continues responsive the current issues demonstrated through increased paid parental leave and expanded provisions for early childhood. These commitments are further evidenced in the steady allocation of city tax dollars to early childhood education.

In a post-fascist Italy, this educational and participatory project emerged by being wide-awake to the realities of the shifting political landscape and using hope to imagine what is possible when you believe school is a public place and site for democracy. Working as a collective, a community, creating reciprocal, trusting relationships, and commitment to civic engagement, policy and structures were developed with the impetus of new experiences, resources, and opportunities rather than market and bottom-lines. In this sense, everyone participates, "individual knowledge is only partial; and that in order to create a project, especially an educational project, everyone's point of view is relevant in dialogue with others" (Cagliari, Barozzi, & Giudici, 2004, p. 29). This is proactive hope. Hope as a collective. Hope as dialogue. Hope as action. Hope as engagement. Hope as responsibility. Hope, in this situation, is the policy directive, it is the doing something about it.

In the educational project of Reggio Emilia, the most visible idea is the image of the child as capable. This is made "explicit and public" (Moss, 2016, p. 171) and underpins policies, structures, and pedagogies (Cagliari et al., 2016). This commitment to the image of the child as capable is what is considered first when making decisions and writing policy in Reggio Emilia. Further, when children are viewed as capable, this constructs how the adults are constructed in this context, calling for the image of a "rich teacher", co-participating and co-constructing knowledge with children, acting as researcher, collaborating with families and the community (Cagliari et al., 2016). This situates the schools "public spaces"—schools as "living centres of open and democratic culture, enriched and informed by social encounters that let them go beyond their ambiguous and false autonomy and centuries-old detachment, and which let them abandon the prejudice of ideological imprinting and authoritarian indoctrination" (Cagliari et al., 2016, p. 180).

For us, this system of schools is where a collective of people just began to do the necessary to work of creating school as a site for democracy, a public place where teaching is always political and connected to the community. It is where we witness students, teachers, and administration all acting as public intellectuals—engaging in complex thinking, conversing and debating, questioning and pondering, disrupting and rethinking, and articulating the relationships between themselves, the local context, and the global community. It is where policies and structures exist and are revised to support the choice of school as a site of democracy, responsive to the community. Together, each of these stakeholders in this system takes on the responsibilities of their role as public intellectual to ensure the school remains part of a democratic society.

Why This Story?

And while this may not be a story about higher education, it is a a story that offers practice of hope in action; it is a story of a community disrupting, resisting, and rethinking towards humanity. It is a story that higher education can take inspiration from in order to see what can be possible.

Constructed with the underlying belief that children, families, and the community are capable, competent, and contributing citizens, for over 80 years with no end in sight, this educational and participatory project has practiced hope and resisted universal educational paradigms that might move from their intentions. Loris Malaguzzi, an educationalist pivotal in this educational project, contributed greatly to this system of public schools,

> Malaguzzi and the schools of Reggio Emilia merit attention from all educationalists who seek to resist the current dominant educational discourse with its intense instrumentality, its reductionist denial of diversity and complexity and its fixation on technical practice, not least the deployment of strong managerial accounting and other human technologies to govern children and adults alike. Moreover, as a system of publicly provided schools inscribed with values of democracy, cooperation and solidarity, Reggio Emilia confronts other shibboleths of neoliberal education orthodoxy, not least its utopian belief in the primacy of private provision, competition and consumer choice. Malaguzzi and the schools of Reggio Emilia are not to be exported and copied, they are (like all education) very much of their time and place. But they show that there are alternatives, not just on paper but in reality.
> (Moss, 2016, p. 168)

This educational and participatory project offers an anti-neoliberal story and they present some interesting elements for consideration as it represents:

1. A community wide awake, aware of their context, the histories, the politics, and the ethics.
2. A community desiring something to be different and willing to imagine what could be otherwise.

3. A community willing to join together and form a collective under a common belief and intention.
4. A community writing and implementing structures and policies to practice the belief and commit to a common intention.
5. A community willing to constantly disrupt, resist, and rethink to ensure the structures and policies continue to reach towards the common intention.
6. A community willing to make their ideas, practices, and challenges public for debate and dialogue.

Being wide-awake, desiring something different, committing to humanity, creating policies and structures, willing to disrupt, resist, and rethink, and make public ideas, practices, challenges—these are all provocations while articulated now in early childhood education in a city in Italy that are appropriate and applicable to higher education. How might the educational project of Reggio Emilia further be impetus for re-imagining higher education? When we exchange the word "community" for "higher education", how might we re-imagine higher education?

1. Higher education is wide awake, aware of its context, the histories, the politics, and the ethics.
2. Higher education desiring something to be different and willing to imagine what could be otherwise.
3. Higher education willing to join together and form a collective under a common belief and intention.
4. Higher education writing and implementing structures and policies to practice the belief and commit to a common intention.
5. Higher education willing to constantly disrupt, resist, and rethink to ensure the structures and policies continue to reach towards the common intention.
6. Higher education willing to make their ideas, practices, and challenges public for debate and dialogue.

How Might This Look?

There was much conversation between us as co-authors on how we might clearly offer to readers a way to start, to just begin this work. As part of the machine of higher education, we know the reliance on words and sometimes the overabundance of words, stops the reading and consideration of new ideas and theories and so we chose to put forth a simple list. A list that might be considered instructions and rather linear. But do not be limited by the numbering or the order. You can enter into the list at any point and move backwords or forwards or sideways. You might begin with what works for your context, your university, your program. And understand that there may be others ways to practice hope beyond what we suggest.

1. Build a Collective with the desire for something to be different
We suggest beginning by building a collective through the practice of hope to position the university as a site of democracy. We see how the collective can work in multiple ways throughout the text and in the educational project of Reggio Emilia. It is a collective willing to engage intellectually with the issues of neoliberalism in higher education and the context where the university is located, using hope to imagine change.

2. Become/be "wide-awake"; find a common intention
In our text, we suggest students, academics, and administrators acting as public intellectuals as a way to disrupt and rethink the neoliberal context in higher education in order position the university as a public space. (This is one way to do this—there are many other ways to do this—what could you imagine for your context?) This repositioning of the key stakeholders within an university community changes priorities and expectations; when the university is a site of democracy, the priority and expectation is about connecting the work of higher education to the local and global context. It is about becoming students, academics, and administrators practicing "wide-awakeness" in their action in the university and beyond.

3. Work as a collective and create policy and structures that support the intention
As a collective, it is necessary to situate this work in the structures and policies of an organization. If current policies and structures do not work, how might these be revised? And what is the underlying commitment of this work? How is it supported in the structures and policies? When these very technical parts of higher education align with the university as site of democracy, they support the work of the student, academic, and administrator as public intellectual. They create the framework for change.

4. Accept that it will be messy
The reality of all of what we suggest throughout this book is that the process is messy. There will be messy entanglements where students, faculty, and administrators act as public intellectuals, being brave enough to question and disrupt. Leading these questions and disruptions to rethinking, brings more mess with negotiation, wonderings, and realities. There will be resistance and push-back. And there will be many days where you find yourself repeating what it means it write policy and structures that support students, academics, and administrators as public intellectuals. But the mess is part of the process–a real process that becomes even more empowering when it is made public.

5. Make it public
Making the thinking, contradictions, and listening public will create more forums, more possibilities for a imagining of what could be in higher education. A strong example of this in the response to our recent presentations at two international conferences, making public our practice of hope and its implications for higher education. Both conferences became the catalyst of expanding the work to significant

discussion around teacher education at universities and building a collective of engaging in the practice of hope beyond our original sites as the higher education institutes representative of three different countries have committed to this work. We are now planning a small conference around these ideas and to build a collective, particularly how teacher education can be rethought by repositioning academics in teacher education as public intellectuals. We are just going to begin.

Returning Back to Our Modest Proposal

Higher education is more than the students, academics, and administrators attending a university. Higher education can be action, as a place that empowers and engage students, academics, and administrators to be in the community and in the world. Higher education is a powerful public space—an active space that can support and further humanity beyond the university walls. Ayers emphasizes (2016),

> The world we need and desire will be forged in action by people struggling for something better, working together in common cause, developing and transforming ourselves as we gather momentum and energy in the hopeful tradition of revolution. We must open our eyes, we must act, and we must rethink and start again. The painstaking work begins, and it can never really be finished.
>
> (p. 234)

And while we witness President Trump making and enforcing policies that separate children from families as a means to deter illegal crossing of borders, we are struck by the critical need for the practice of hope. A simple overturning by President Trump of the "zero-tolerance" policy of criminal prosecution of adults crossing the border illegally could ensure children staying with families. Yet this solution is not pursued. These acts remind us of Swift's (1729) answer to poverty of the Irish by "selling their children as food for the wealthy." Swift's absurd ideas were imagined in order to shock and shame England and Ireland into taking action. In this case, the absurdity of some of our current decision-making and actions are real. And the shock and shame generated through this horrific situation does not even register and humanity is far from consideration. Rather, perpetuation of self (perhaps Trump himself) and distraction from equity, social justice, and human rights ensues.

Our intention in re-imagining *A Modest Proposal* was to provoke our own thinking to more action. Our act of re-imagining also further cements our realisation that we are also cogs in the neoliberal machine situated in higher education. Be awake to this positioning of ourselves as an academic and an administrator as well as what could be possible in universities. It is the tension between understanding our role in perpetuating neoliberalism and resisting and rethinking that the practice of hope emerged. Hope is a framework for action; it is how we work "for something better." The practice of hope is how we have come together, a small collective building and gaining momentum as others think with us and challenge us. In the re-imagining of *A Modest Proposal* and the subsequent conversations and research we were offered new possibilities, some setbacks, and further understandings of the reality of the higher education. Our intent is that the practice of hope might be a way for students, academics, and administrators to open their eyes, act, rethink, and start again. Much like Ayers (2016) so eloquently states, "The painstaking work begins, and it can never really be finished" (p. 234). Yet, we remember that never being finished is part of a courageous and proper response to neoliberalism in the university and the provocation for constantly imagining and implementing hope and possibilities.

References

Ayers, W. (2016). *Demand the impossible*. Chicago: Haymarket Books.
Cagliari, P., Barozzi, A., & Giudici, C. (2004). Thoughts, theories and experiences: For an educational project with participation. *Children in Europe, 6*, 28–30.
Cagliari, P., Castegnetti, M., Giudici, C., Rinaldi, C., Vecchi, V., & Moss, P. (2016). *Loris Malaguzzi and the schools of Reggio Emilia: A selection of his writings and speeches 1945–1993*. London, England: Routledge.
Dahlberg, G., & Moss, P. (2006). Introduction: our Reggio Emilia. In C. Rinaldi(Ed.), *In dialogue with Reggio Emilia: Listening, researching and learning* (pp. 1-22). New York: Routledge.
Moss, P. (2016). Loris Malaguzzi and the schools of Reggio Emilia: Provocation and hope for a renewed public education. *Improving Schools, 19*(2), 167–176.
Swift, J. (1729). *A modest proposal*. Retrieved from http://www.gutenberg.org/files/1080/1080-h/1080-h.htm.

Printed in the United States
By Bookmasters